TO TEACHERS & PARENTS

This book, *California Early History*, was written as a simplified, yet complete, resource book for you to use in your classroom or at home. The activities can be used as a supplement to your regular history curriculum; or it can be used as your primary history text.

There are twelve separate sections in this book. The first eleven sections cover California's history from the discovery days through statehood. Each of these sections is written in such a way that it can be used individually — without going in order — or they can all be completed in order (which we recommend). The sections are arranged chronologically in the book. Section twelve is the answer keys.

We have included four unique sections in this history book. These are the sections on Californians of Native American, Mexican, African and Asian descent. We think this will help students understand that the people are more important than dates and events in the growth and development of a nation or state. Moreover, we hope they will realize that without people and their cultural, moral and religious beliefs and differences the history written here would probably be different. In these sections we have done our best to present the truth about events and attitudes of the times, while trying to keep the text meaningful, easy to understand and brief. We believe our research is accurate. We tried not to offend any of the cultural groups discussed. It was impossible to present all of the cultural/ethnic groups that have made California a great state. If we have omitted your nationality or any events you think should have been included, please accept our apology. (Write us and we will consider including them in our next edition.) It is our hope that you, as the teacher, will present the cultural customs, contributions and heritage of these and other nationalities in greater detail.

New vocabulary words are introduced at the beginning of each new section. Students should look the words up in the dictionary and write short definitions for each of the words. They could even write the words in their own sentences in addition to looking them up. It is suggested that teachers or aides discuss the meanings of the words before the lessons are actually begun. This will help make sure that the meanings are understood by the students. This will help your students grasp the events and concepts being discussed in each section.

The lessons are reinforced with maps, exercises, review questions and bonus activities. *Bonus Activities* are at the end of each section. Students will always need to use an additional resource to complete these activities. Teachers should decide if the students are required to do the research in order to complete these bonus activities. Please feel free to add your own ideas in order to expand on the ones given in this book.

We hope you and your students enjoy using this book.

Randy L. Womack
Author

Notes & Doodles

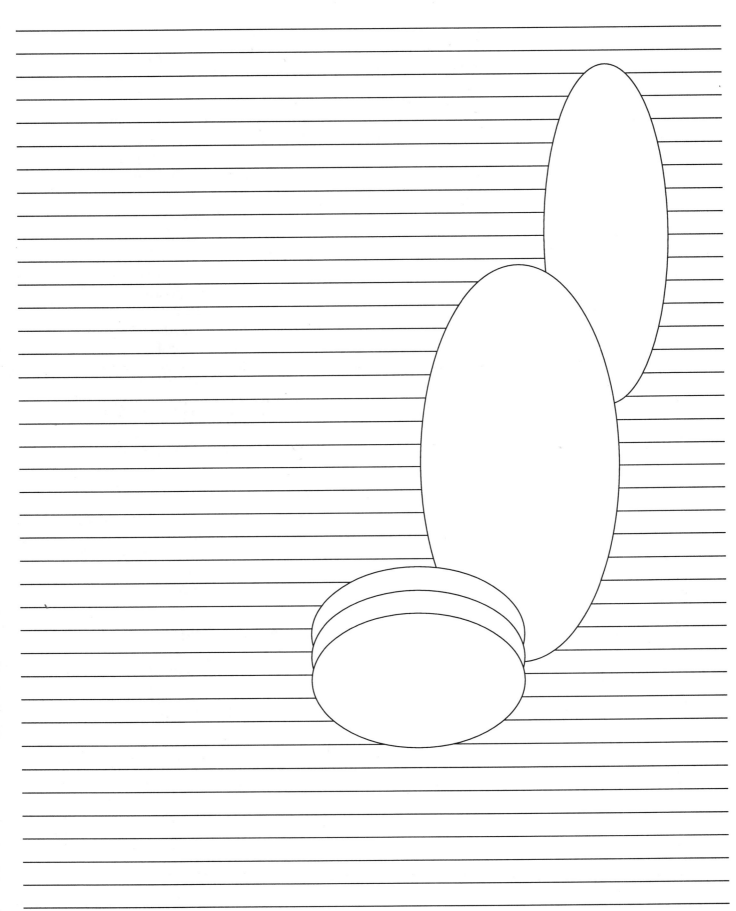

California Early History

Maps

Lessons

Vocabulary

Review Questions

Bonus Activities
(Research Projects)

WRITTEN BY
RANDY L. WOMACK, M.ED.
LEARNING DISABILITIES & BEHAVIOR DISORDERS

ILLUSTRATED BY
CHRISTINA "CHRIS" LEW

PUBLISHED BY

G.E.C. PUBLICATIONS
"LEADING THE WAY IN CREATIVE EDUCATIONAL MATERIALS" ™

857 LAKE BLVD. ❖ REDDING, CALIFORNIA 96003
www.goldened.com

This book is dedicated to Keith Beery, Director of the Respect Institute, researcher, educator, author, and friend. I am grateful to him for his contributions to this book. He treats all people, regardless of their education, social status, or ethnic heritage with respect and consideration. All of us could learn a lot from Keith.

If you would like to introduce your students to California geography, or the Spanish/Catholic Missions in California, we have books and posters available. They are written in the same easy-to-use-and-read format as this *California Early History* book. See the ad sheets in the back of this book for information regarding these and other materials we offer. Please contact your local retail outlet and they will be happy to order as many copies as you need. If you do not have a retail outlet in your area, please contact the publisher directly using the address or phone number below.

Copyright ©1990 **Randy L. Womack**
Updated ©2004 ALL RIGHTS RESERVED – PRINTED IN U.S.A
PUBLISHED BY GOLDEN EDUCATIONAL CENTER
857 LAKE BLVD. ❖ REDDING, CALIFORNIA 96003
1.800.800.1791 ❖ FAX 1.530.244.5939

TM

ISBN 1-56500-027-7

California
Early History
Section Contents

Vocabulary Words ❖ Maps ❖ Questions
☆☆ Bonus Activities
Included in the First Ten Sections of This Book

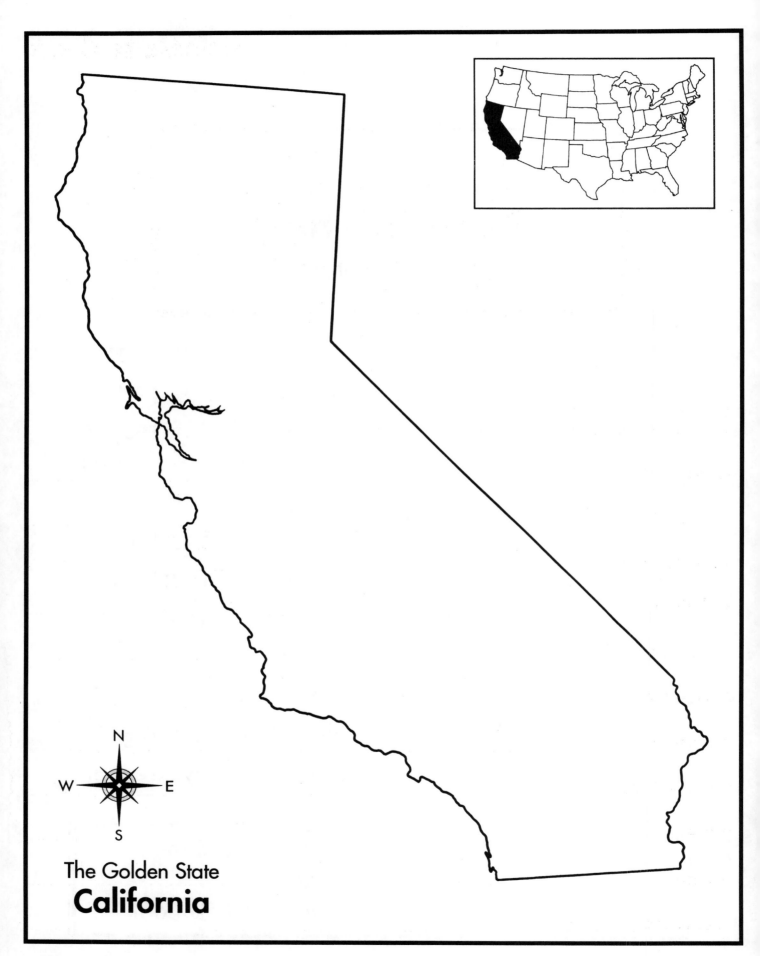

The Golden State
California

California Early History
Native Americans

New Words to Learn:
Find the words in a dictionary and write the meanings on the line.

1. **culture:**_____

2. **customs:**_____

3. **descendant:**_____

4. **dialect:**_____

5. **environment:**_____

6. **identity:**_____

7. **migrate:**_____

8. **stereotype:**_____

9. **theory:**_____

10. **tribe** (tribal):_____

11. **unique:**_____

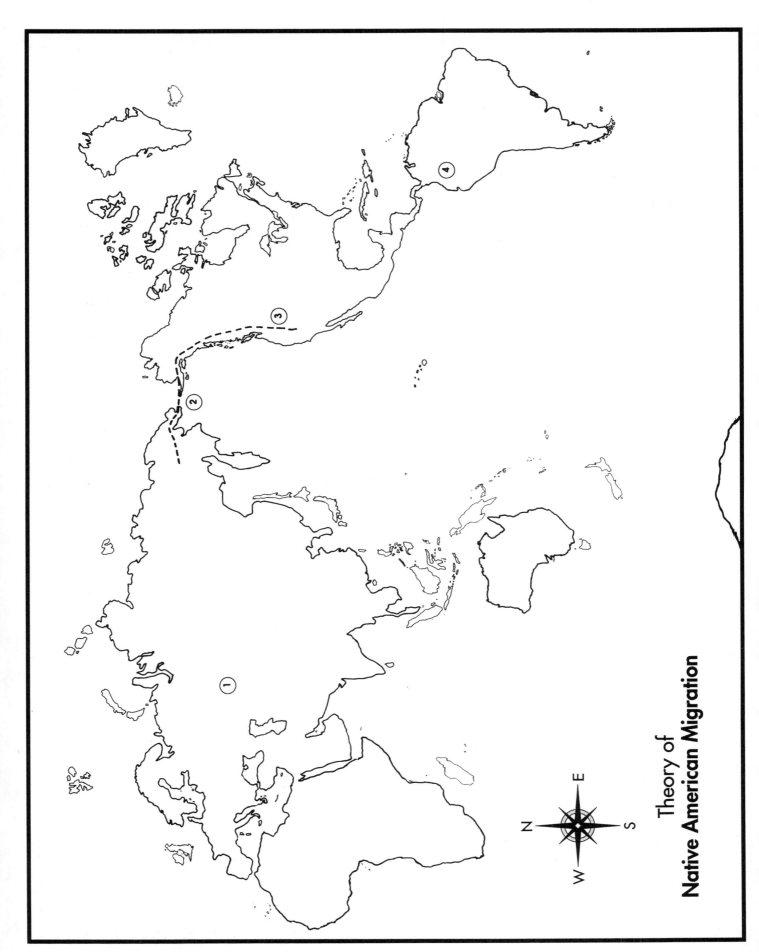

Theory of
Native American Migration

California
Native Americans

The First to Live in California

The first people to live in the area that is now California were American Indians of various tribes. Nobody knows for sure how they got to this region of the world. One **theory** is that maybe there was a *land bridge* across the Bering Sea near Alaska. This bridge could have allowed people to **migrate** from Asia to North America. However, neither scientists, nor anybody else knows for sure.

In 1492, Christopher Columbus was sailing from Spain. He was looking for a faster and easier route to India. He happened upon the continent of North America and discovered the first North American peoples. Columbus thought he was in India so he called the people living there *Indians*. Because of this mistaken **identity**, today, many **descendants** of the first Americans prefer to be called *Native Americans* or *American Indians*.

Ever since Columbus' time, a mistake that is often made by non-Indian people is to **stereotype** American Indians. It is important to remember that Native American groups developed **many different ways of life**. These ways of living were most often based on the **environment** and on the type of land where the people lived. The native people from each area of the United States developed their own **unique culture**. Each culture matched the environment that surrounded their homes.

Do these things using the map provided.

1. Trace over the broken line (– – – – – – – –) with a pen or pencil to show the path that the first people to come to America might have taken.

2. Write **Asia** ①, **Bering Sea** ②, **North America** ③ and **South America** ④ by the correct number.

3. Color your map as nicely as you can.

☆☆ Bonus Activity
On another piece of paper, draw a picture of how *you* think some of the Native Americans lived. You can draw it the way you imagine it might have been. You can also find a picture of their homes in another book.

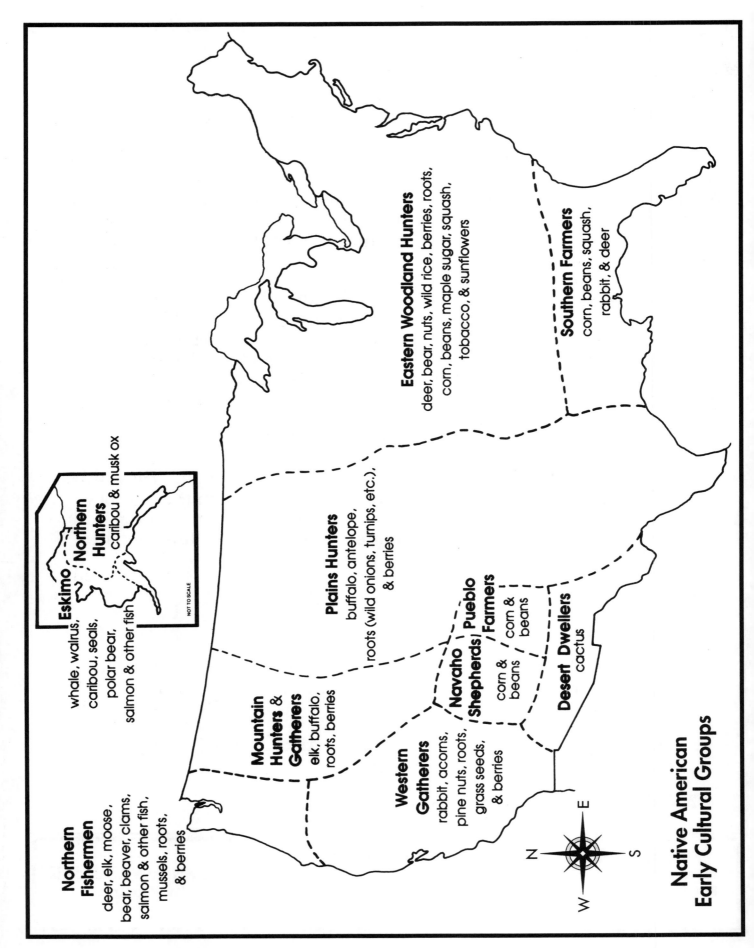

Native American Early Cultural Groups

Eskimo
Northern Hunters
caribou & musk ox

NOT TO SCALE

Eastern Woodland Hunters
deer, bear, nuts, wild rice, berries, roots, corn, beans, maple sugar, squash, tobacco, & sunflowers

Southern Farmers
corn, beans, squash, rabbit, & deer

Plains Hunters
buffalo, antelope, roots (wild onions, turnips, etc.), & berries

Pueblo Farmers
corn & beans

Navaho Shepherds
corn & beans

Desert Dwellers
cactus

Mountain Hunters & Gatherers
elk, buffalo, roots, berries

Western Gatherers
rabbit, acorns, pine nuts, roots, grass seeds, & berries

Northern Fishermen
deer, elk, moose, bear, beaver, clams, salmon & other fish, mussels, roots, & berries

N E S W

California Native Americans

Name _____

Date _____

Early Cultural Groups

Long ago, American Indians did not think of themselves as *Indian*. They saw themselves as **tribal** people, identified by a tribal name — *Hopi, Sioux, Snohomish, Iowa, Illinois* and many others. In fact, there were about 200 different languages spoken by Native Americans all over the continent of North America. Depending on what nature provided in their particular area, the groups of American Indians built their homes differently. They ate different types of food, made and used different kinds of tools, developed different governments and **customs**.

The map on the left shows the ten early cultural areas of Native Americans living in the United States. Generally, most of the tribes living within each of the areas could be grouped as the map shows. They are grouped here as farmers, gatherers, and hunters because that shows their main source of food and the culture they developed.

Most American Indians lived what we would consider a very simple life style. Many of the tribes hunted or gathered their food. Some were farmers. They all lived off of the land. Most of them got along with the other tribes in their area.

The California Indians were primarily *gatherers*. The acorn from the oak tree was the basic food of their diet. They also gathered seeds, berries, and nuts. They did some hunting and fishing.

Do these things using the map provided.

1. Pick 3 of the cultural areas on the map and draw a picture of at least one of the foods they ate. You can use another piece of paper if you would like. Just make sure you label the picture with the correct cultural group.

2. Color the *Western Gatherers* your favorite color.

3. Color the rest of the cultural groups any other combination of colors. Use a different color for each cultural group.

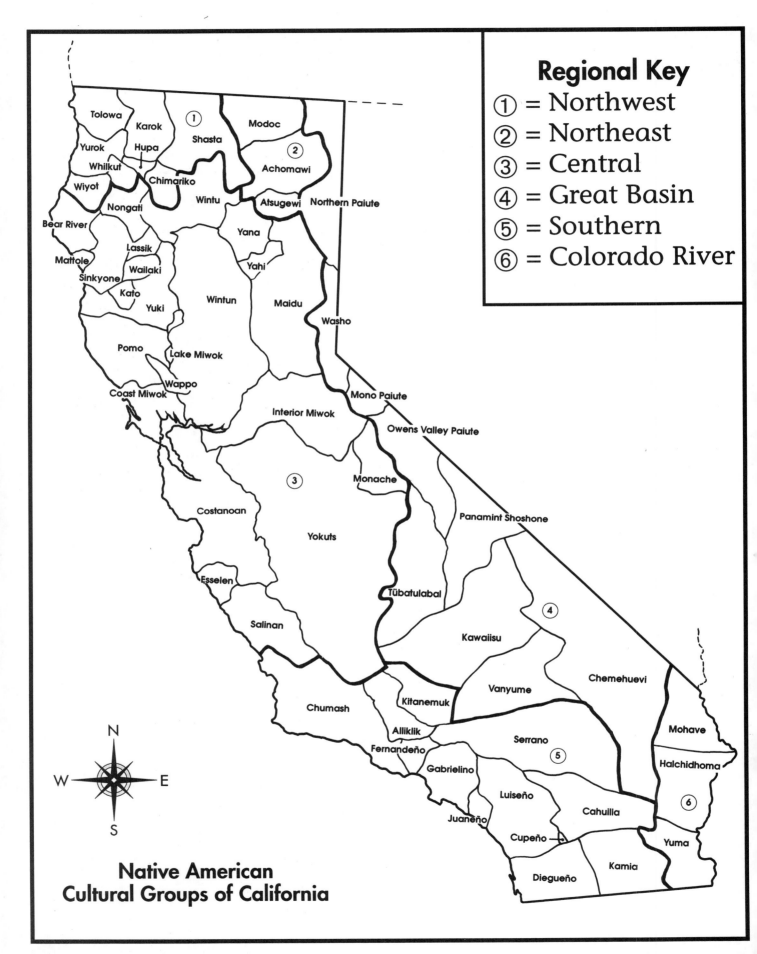

Regional Key

① = Northwest
② = Northeast
③ = Central
④ = Great Basin
⑤ = Southern
⑥ = Colorado River

Tolowa
Karok
Shasta
①
Modoc
Yurok
Hupa
Whilkut
Chimariko
Wiyot
Nongati
Wintu
Atsugewi
②
Achomawi
Northern Paiute
Bear River
Lassik
Mattole
Wailaki
Yana
Sinkyone
Kato
Yahi
Yuki
Wintun
Maidu
Pomo
Lake Miwok
Washo
Wappo
Coast Miwok
Interior Miwok
Mono Paiute
Owens Valley Paiute
③
Monache
Costanoan
Yokuts
Panamint Shoshone
Esselen
Salinan
Tübatulabal
④
Kawaiisu
Chemehuevi
Vanyume
Chumash
Kitanemuk
Alliklik
Fernandeño
Serrano
Mohave
⑤
Gabrielino
Halchidhoma
Luiseño
Cahuilla
Juaneño
⑥
Cupeño
Yuma
Kamia
Diegueño

N
W   E
S

Native American
Cultural Groups of California

Cultural Groups of California

The California Indians made beautiful baskets that they used for cooking and gathering food. Their weaving skills were so good that they could boil water in their baskets. They also wove beautiful designs into their blankets. Sometimes they made clay pottery with nice designs.

Deserts and high mountains separated the California Indians from each other and from tribes further East. Because of this geography, the California Indians had very little contact with other tribes. Each had its own **dialect** or language. The Indians of California were not warlike people. They rarely had wars between themselves. However, the *Mohave* and *Yuma* tribes sometimes had to fight outsiders.

The *Hupa* people lived in the far northwestern part of what is now California. The *Maidu* lived in the central section, and the *Yuma* lived in the south. The *Pomo* people lived in the territory that is now Mendocino, Sonoma and Lake counties, a little north of San Francisco. Some of the other American Indians who lived in the California region included the *Míwok*, *Modoc* and *Mohave* tribes.

The Modoc War (1872-1873) was the last effort made by Native Californians to maintain their way of life before other people came to the area. ☆☆ Using another resource, write a report on this war or any of the Native American wars you are interested in.

Do these things using the map provided.

1. Find the seven California Indian tribes mentioned on this page and color them orange or gold. *Be careful; some lived in more than one area.*

2. Choose a different color to use for each of the other regional areas. (Example: Color the Hupa area gold and the rest of the entire Northwest area a different color.) Choose a new color for each region.

California
Native Americans

Name _____

Date _____

REVIEW QUESTIONS

Write the correct answer in the space provided.

1. Ever since Columbus discovered America, what is one mistake about Native Americans that other people often make?_____

2. Explain the *land bridge* theory. _____
_____

3. Explain how Native Americans came to be called *Indians*._____
_____

4. California Native Americans got most of their food by _____ it.

Circle the best answer to each question.

5. What determined the way a tribe lived?
      a. its leader   b. its environment   c. its customs

6. How many Native American languages were spoken in North America?
      a. 2   b. 20   c. 200   d. 2,000

7. All Native American tribes…
      a. lived off the land   b. fished   3. hunted   d. farmed

Write the correct (best) answer on the line from the list of bold words.

Hupa_____   **Northern Border**

Míwok_____   **North San Francisco**

Maidu_____   **Southern**

Pomo _____   **Northwestern**

Modoc_____   **South Pacific Coast**

Mohave _____   **Central**

Yuma _____   **Southeastern**

☆☆ **Bonus Activity**
On another piece of paper, explain why *you* think
Native Americans do not want to be stereotyped by other people.

California
Early History
Mexican Americans

New Words to Learn:

Find the words in a dictionary and write the meanings on the line.

1. **astronomy:** _____

2. **brutal:** _____

3. **civilization:** _____

4. **colony:** _____

5. **empire:** _____

6. **heritage:** _____

7. **influence:** _____

8. **irrigation:** _____

9. **technique:** _____

Name _____

Date _____

Color the drawing of
an Aztec pyramid.

Aztec Calendar

This stone calendar was used
by the Aztecs in ceremonies
honoring their sun god —
Tonatiuh. His face is carved in
the center of the stone. The
other carvings are religious
symbols and symbols for the
days of the month.

**Color the drawing of
an Aztec pyramid.**

California
Mexican Americans

Name _____

Date _____

Aztec Empire

Mexican Americans have a history that is different from any other group of people in America. Over several hundred years, they have been formed by the combination of two different cultures and nations. One culture was the American Indian and the other was the Spanish settlers who arrived in what is known today as Mexico. Their Indian roots make them descendants of the oldest and most highly developed civilization on the North American continent. Their Spanish **heritage** gives them a close relationship with the rich culture of Europe.

One of the strongest Indian **influences** was that of the mighty Aztec **civilization**. The Aztecs ruled the **empire** of Mexico in the 1400's and early 1500's, before any Spaniards arrived on the continent. The Aztec culture had reached a level of development that equalled or surpassed that of many European countries.

The Aztecs had built large well-organized cities with pyramids, temples, libraries, and schools. They even had a zoo. They had developed a written language, a system of mathematics, scientific farming **techniques**, **astronomy**, and a method of **irrigation** that was as good as any other in the entire world. Their poetry and literature were very good and the Aztecs had constructed theaters where plays were presented.

> **Color the map showing the Aztec empire.**

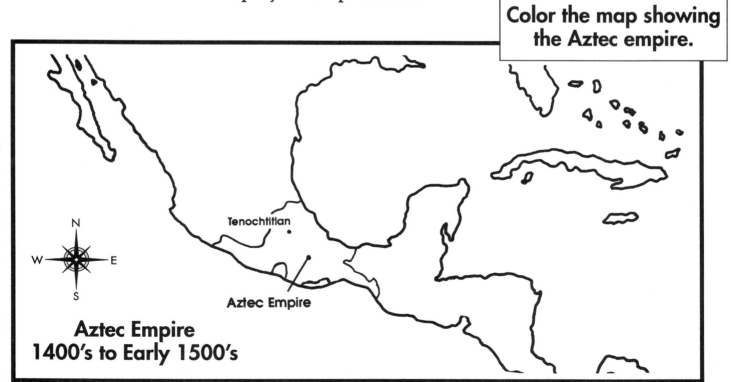

Tenochtitlan

Aztec Empire

**Aztec Empire
1400's to Early 1500's**

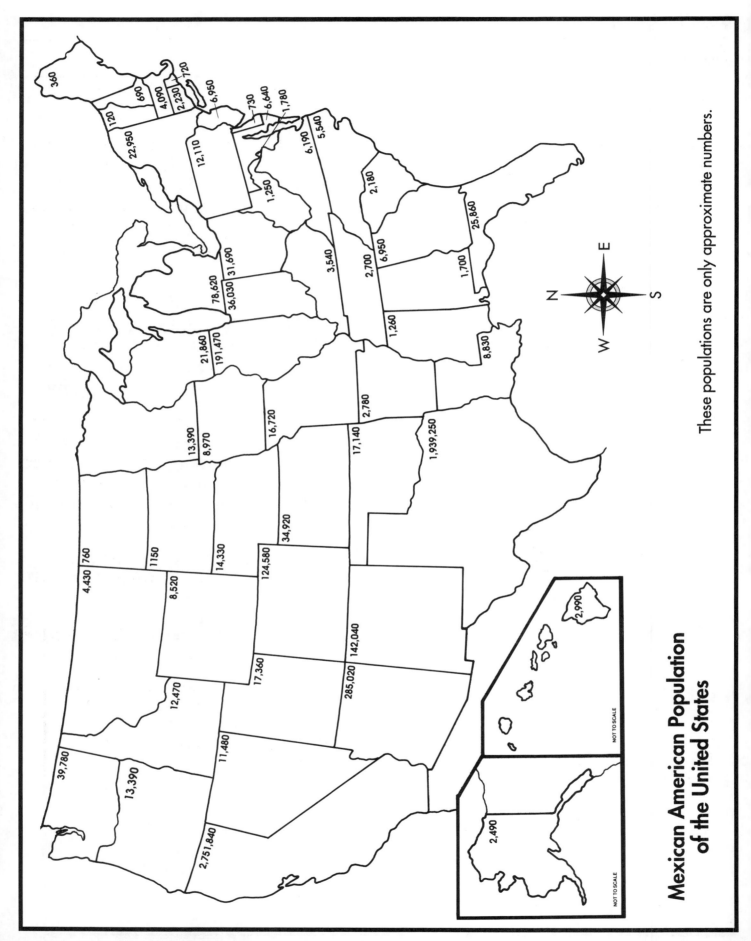

These populations are only approximate numbers.

Mexican American Population of the United States

NOT TO SCALE

NOT TO SCALE

Spanish Colony

The Spanish explorers were very impressed by the wealth and beauty of the Aztecs' capital city of Tenochtitlan. It was built in the same place where Mexico City stands today. Cortez was the leader of a Spanish expedition that came upon the great city. The Aztec leader, Montezuma II, welcomed Cortez and his men. Montezuma gave them many gifts and lots of gold. To the Aztecs, gold was a thing of beauty, and they used it to create beautiful works of art. For Cortez and the Europeans, gold was a sign of wealth and power.

Cortez wanted to expand the Spanish empire, so he decided to defeat the Aztecs and take their gold and land for Spain. After two years of **brutal** warfare, the Spaniards finally managed to destroy one of the most highly developed civilizations in the world at that time.

The Spanish visitors who came to America were different from the other Europeans who came. The Spaniards did not intend to become permanent settlers. English ships would bring whole families of settlers to America. Most of the Spanish ships only carried men. Those Spaniards who did settle in America took Native Americans as their wives. Their children became *mestizos,* or a mixture of Spanish and Indian blood. This mixing of two nations and two cultures over many years created a new cultural group, the Mexicans.

With the defeat of the Aztecs, Mayans and other Indian groups, Mexico became a **colony** of Spain. It was called *New Spain.* A new culture grew out of combining different elements of the Indian and Spanish ways of life.

In search of gold, the people of Mexico began to move north into the areas that would later become Texas, New Mexico, Colorado, Arizona and California.

Today there is a growing movement toward greater strength and pride among Mexican American people. A term that refers to people of Spanish ancestry is *Hispanic.* Mexican American people also use the term *Raza* as a name for all people of mixed Spanish and Indian blood in both North and South America.

Do these things using the map provided.

1. Write the names of all the states showing the Mexican American population of each. *You will probably have to look at another resource.*

2. Color your map *after* you label the states.

California
Mexican Americans

REVIEW QUESTIONS

Write the correct answer in the space provided.

1. Tell how the mighty Aztec civilization had developed in the 1400's. _____
_____
_____

2. How are Mexican Americans different from any other group of people
in the United States? _____
_____

3. What impressed the Spanish explorers about the Aztec capital
of Tenochtitlan? _____

4. Explain how Cortez planned to expand the Spanish empire._____
_____

5. Explain what is meant by the term *mestizo.* _____
_____

6. Tell what you think was right or wrong about the way Cortez and his
soldiers treated the Aztecs and other Native Americans. _____
_____
_____

Circle the best answer to each question.

7. After the defeat of the Aztecs, Mexico became known as...
    a. Independent   b. Mestizos   c. New Spain

8. Tenochtitlan was built in the area that is known as...
    a. Mexico City   b. Montezuma   c. Beautiful

9. What were the Mexican people looking for when they moved north?
    a. Independence   b. Texas and other states   c. Gold

☆☆ Bonus Activity
Using another resource book, write a report on the Aztecs or Mayan people and/or
civilizations. Make maps of their empires and pictures of things they made or used.

New Words to Learn:
Find the words in a dictionary and write the meanings on the line.

1. **contrary:**_____

2. **greed:** _____

3. **ignorant:**_____

4. **indenture:** _____

5. **kidnap:** _____

6. **phase:** _____

7. **primitive:** _____

8. **profit:** _____

9. **prosper:** _____

10. **servant:** _____

11. **slave:** _____

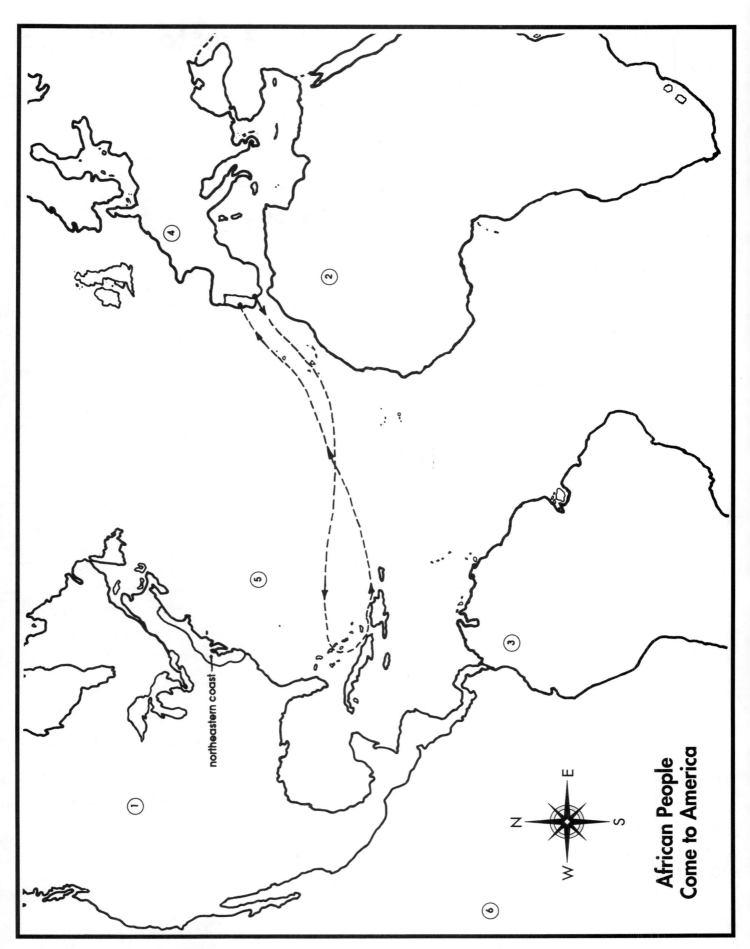

northeastern coast

African People Come to America

California
Black Americans

Name _____

Date _____

Coming to America

Contrary to what many people may think, the first Black people to come to America were not **slaves**. The earliest recorded Black man to come to the Americas was on the last trip Columbus made in 1502. His name was Diego el Negro. Several more black explorers were also on the crews of Francisco Coronado, Cabeza de Vaca and Vasco Balboa. These Spanish explorers led some of the first expeditions to what are the American continents today.

The earliest known Black settlers in the United States came in 1619. They came and settled on the northeastern coast, in New England. From the map, it is easy to see why they came to the East Coast rather than the West. These first Black settlers were **indentured servants** not slaves.

Records also show that the earliest Black settlers from the United States to make their way to California included John Gibson. He was a sailor who came to the town of Monterey. In 1816, a man named Bob and one named Thomas Doak jumped ship and settled in California.

Indentured servants would agree to serve and work for a family or company for 5-7 years after they arrived in America. They agreed to this in exchange for the "master" paying for their voyage to America. (However, many of these people were captured and sold as "servants" against their will.) At the end of the agreed-upon length of serving, the servants would be free to live as they wished. This was the only way many of the Black people could afford to come to America, the *land of opportunity*. It worked out well for both the master and the servant. The indentured servants were treated much better than the slaves were treated.

Do these things using the map provided.

1. Trace over the broken line (– – – – – – – –) with a pen or pencil to show the route Columbus took to America.

2. Color the northeastern coast of North America, where the first Black settlers arrived, gold or orange.

3. Write **North America** ①, **Africa** ②, **South America** ③, **Europe** ④, **Atlantic Ocean** ⑤ and **Pacific Ocean** ⑥ by the correct number.

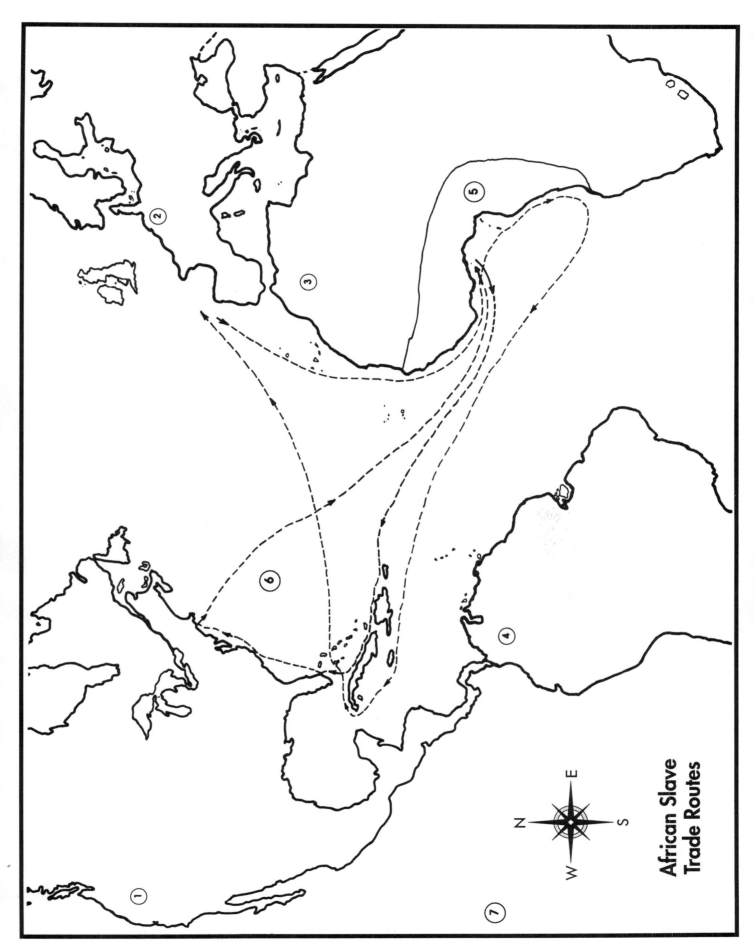

African Slave
Trade Routes

California
Black Americans

Name _____

Date _____

First Black Settlers

Unlike the early Black explorers and settlers, most of the Black people who came to America between 1600 and 1800 were brought here against their will. They were **kidnapped** from their African homes and forced to live out the rest of their lives in slavery.

Most of the slaves were taken from West Africa. Because of its location on the Atlantic coast, ships could easily load the kidnapped people and sail for America. These kidnapped Black people were not **ignorant** or **primitive** people. In fact, they had developed very rich, highly organized civilizations that had been growing and **prospering** for hundreds of years. Some of the cultures had developed highly organized schools, banks and businesses.

The slave trade was introduced because it produced huge **profits** for the businessmen of Europe, North America and the West Indies. Slaves were needed for free labor on the cotton, coffee and tobacco plantations. Slavery in both North and South America proved to be the main factor that destroyed some of the great African civilizations. The **greedy** merchants who loved money, power and themselves more than the dignity and cultures of other people, kidnapped at least 10 million Black people over a period of 300 years and sold them into slavery.

It is known that almost half the founding adults of Los Angeles were either all or partly of Black descent. The population of Black people grew from about 1,000 to 2,200 in 1850-1852.

Black people were part of every **phase** of the *Westward Movement*. Some were trappers, hunters, explorers and settlers. Several Black individuals had influences in the growth, development and history of California. However, the large number of Native Americans, Mexicans and Asians had a greater influence on California's early history. The geographical location of North America, Asia and Africa was a major reason for the small number of Black people who migrated to California in the early days.

Do these things using the map provided.

1. Trace over the broken line (– – – – – – – –) with a pen or pencil to show the routes that the slave trade ships took from Africa.

2. Write **North America** ①, **Europe** ②, **Africa** ③, **South America** ④, **West Africa** ⑤, **Atlantic Ocean** ⑥ and **Pacific Ocean** ⑦ by the correct number. Color your map as neatly as you can.

California
Black Americans

Name _____

Date _____

REVIEW QUESTIONS

Write the correct answer in the space provided.

1. Explain why the first Black people to settle in the United States came to the East Coast rather than the West Coast. _____
_____

2. Why was *slave trade* introduced in the Americas? _____
_____

3. Explain what the term *indentured servant* means. _____
_____
_____
_____

4. From 1600 to 1800, why did most of the Black people come to America?
_____

5. Describe how *you* would have felt had you been one of the African people to be kidnapped and forced to come to America as a slave. _____
_____
_____
_____
_____

Write the correct (best) answer on the line from the list of bold words.

Sold Into Slavery _____

First Black Explorer _____

Indentured Servants _____

Organized Civilizations _____

New England _____

Free Labor _____

African People

Worked for Their Freedom

10 Million African People

Columbus

Diego el Negro

Slaves

Earliest Black Settlers

☆☆ **Bonus Activity**
Using another resource book, write a report on Slavery, West Africa, African Cultures, African Art or Early African Civilizations. Include pictures and maps to go with your report.

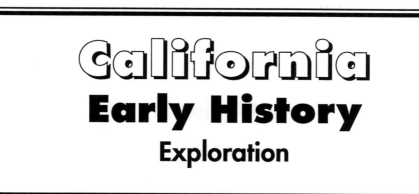

California Early History
Exploration

New Words to Learn:

Find the words in a dictionary and write the meanings on the line.

1. **claim:** _____

2. **coast:** _____

3. **colonize:** _____

4. **crew:** _____

5. **expedition:** _____

6. **explore** (explorer): _____

7. **route:** _____

8. **tale:** _____

9. **territory:** _____

10. **voyage:** _____

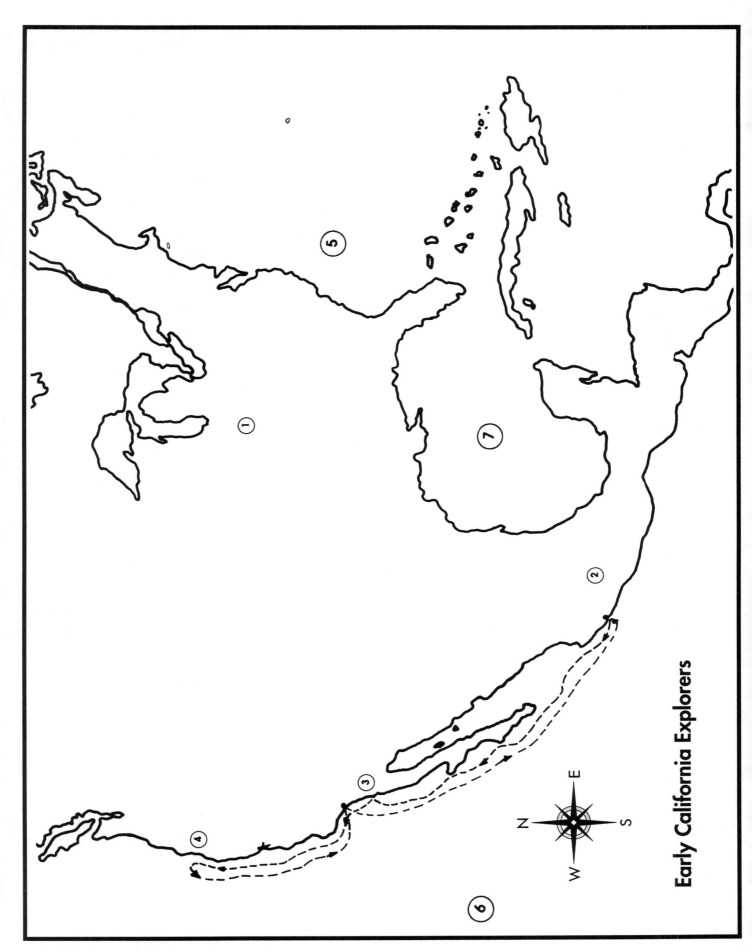

Early California Explorers

California
Exploration

Name _____

Date _____

Juan Rodríguez Cabrillo

Juan Rodríguez Cabrillo was a Portuguese **explorer** employed by Spain. He was sent by Spain to look for cities of riches and a water **route** to Asia through North America. He was probably the first European to see the **coast** of what is now California.

In 1542, Cabrillo sailed north from *New Spain*. (This is the region of today's Mexico. It was a Spanish colony in the 1500's.) He sailed along the Pacific coast. On September 28, 1542 he sailed into a bay of water. He named it *San Miguel Bay*. Later, the name was changed to *San Diego*, as it is still known today.

Cabrillo and his crew sailed north along the coast of California. He broke either his arm or leg on the trip. (It is not known for sure which bone he broke.) There was not proper medical care on his ship and he became very sick. In January of 1543, he died from an infection caused by the broken bone.

Before he died, Cabrillo asked his men to continue the **expedition**. Their new captain was Bartolome Ferrelo. It is believed that they sailed as far north as present-day Oregon. They found no *cities of gold* or waterway to Asia. The ship and **crew** returned to New Spain hungry and sick.

Do these things using the map provided.

1. Trace over the broken line (– – – – – – – –) with a pen or pencil to show the route that Juan Rodríguez Cabrillo and his men took while exploring the coast of California.

2. Write **North America** ①, **New Spain** ②, **San Diego** ③, **Oregon** ④, **Atlantic Ocean** ⑤, **Pacific Ocean** ⑥ and **Gulf of Mexico** ⑦ by the correct number.

3. Color your map as neatly as you can.

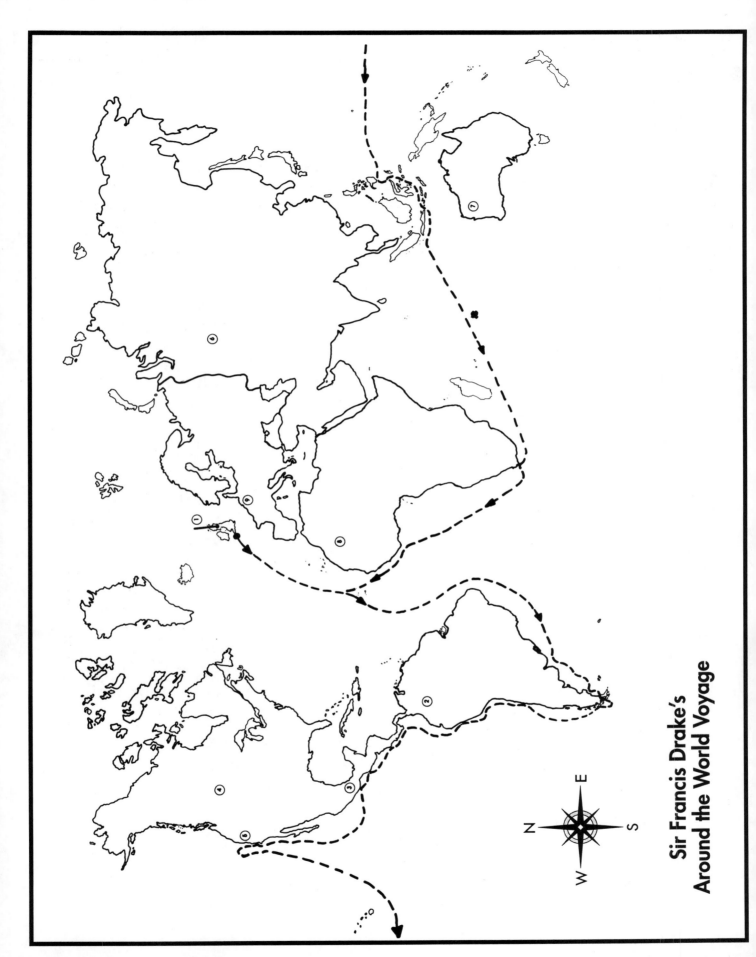

Sir Francis Drake's
Around the World Voyage

California
Exploration

Name _____

Date _____

Sir Francis Drake

In 1579, Francis Drake followed a route along the coast of California in his ship, the *Golden Hind*. He was an English explorer, making his famous **voyage** around the world. (His voyage took three years, from 1577-1580.) He was the first Englishman to sail around the world. Drake **claimed** the land for England and named it *New Albion*. On June 17th, Drake's ship made an emergency landing on the coast of California. The place where the ship anchored is now called *Drake's Bay*.

Drake's stop in California made the Spanish government afraid that they might lose the **territory** to England. For the next 60 years the Spanish government sent many ships to explore the California coast.

Sebastían Vizcaíno

In 1602, the Spanish explorer, Sebastían Vizcaíno, led one of the trips along the coast of California. He renamed many of the places Cabrillo had named in 1542. When Vizcaíno arrived back to New Spain, he sent a report to the King of Spain. In the report, Vizcaíno strongly urged the King to **colonize** California.

The region was named *California* by these early explorers. It was most likely named after a treasure island in a popular Spanish **tale**. The tale was in the book, *Las Sergas de Esplandían*. The book was written by Garcia Ordóñez de Montalvo in the early 1500's.

Do these things using the map provided.

1. Trace over the broken line (– – – – – – – –) with a pen or pencil to show the route that Sir Francis Drake and his men took around the world.

2. Write, **England** ①, **South America** ②, **New Spain** ③, **North America** ④, **Drake's Bay** ⑤, **Asia** ⑥, **Australia** ⑦, **Africa** ⑧ and **Europe** ⑨ by the correct number.

3. Color your map as nicely as you can. Make each continent a different color.

California Exploration

REVIEW QUESTIONS

Write the correct answer in the space provided.

1. What did the Europeans call Mexico in the 1500's? _____

2. Tell what you think Sebastían Vizcaíno said in his message to the King of Spain after his trip along California's coast. _____
_____

3. Explain how Juan Rodríguez Cabrillo died. _____
_____

4. What was *San Miguel Bay* later named? _____

5. The explorer, Juan Rodríguez Cabrillo, and his men were looking for what two things? _____
_____

6. What is the famous voyage that Sir Francis Drake is *most* famous for?
_____

Circle the best answer to each question.

7. For which country did Sir Francis Drake claim the coast of California?
    a. Spain   b. Portugal   c. England   d. Mexico

8. The first *known* European to see the coast of California was...
    a. Bartolome Ferrelo   b. Juan Cabrillo   c. Sir Francis Drake

9. Which explorer renamed many of the places in California?
    a. Sebastían Vizcaíno   b. Sir Francis Drake   c. Juan Cabrillo

10. Which country sent the most ships to explore the coast of California?
    a. Portugal   b. Spain   c. England   d. Mexico   e. France

---

☆☆ Bonus Activity
Using another resource book, write a report on one of the explorers you have read about, or choose a different one. Make maps of their voyages and pictures of their ships.

New Words to Learn:

Find the words in a dictionary and write the meanings on the line.

1. **abundance:** _____

2. **cartographer:** _____

3. **continent:** _____

4. **establish:** _____

5. **Jesuit:** _____

6. **mission** (noun): _____

7. **missionary:** _____

8. **organize:** _____

9. **province:** _____

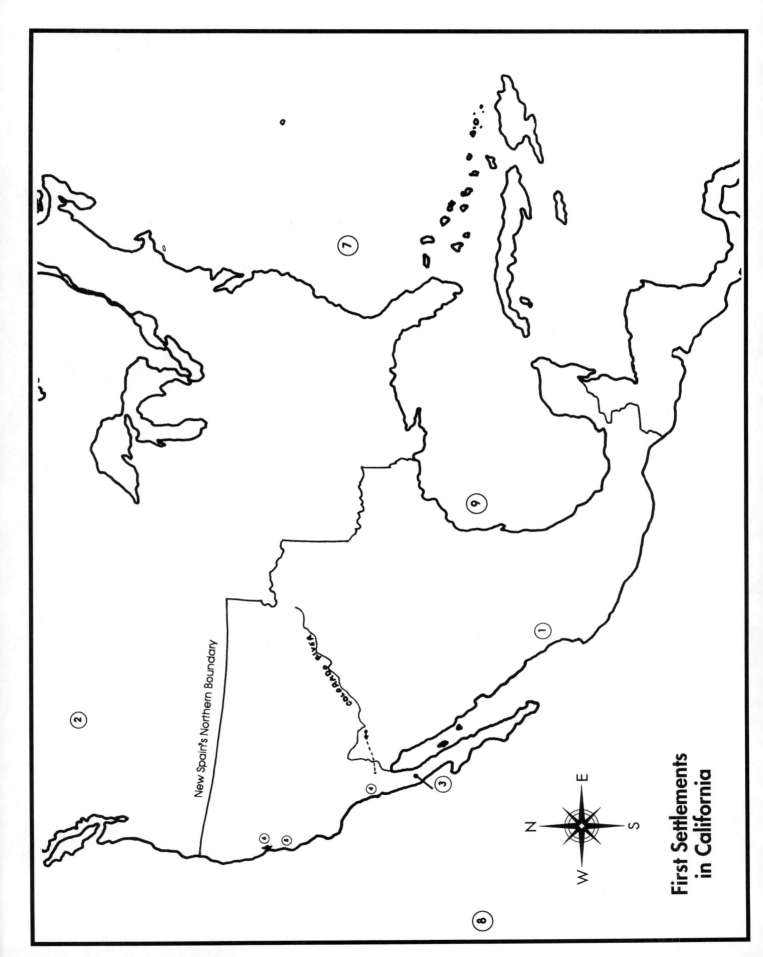

First Settlements in California

California
Settlements

Jesuits

In 1701, Father Eusebio Francisco Kino, a **Jesuit** priest, crossed the Colorado River and went into California. He wanted to do **missionary** work with the Native Americans living in the area. He had been building **missions** in what is now Arizona. Father Kino was a good **cartographer** (map maker). He showed that California was part of the North American **continent**. The Spanish government forced the Jesuits out of the territory.

Spanish

The King of Spain ordered **settlements** to be **established** in California. Beginning in 1697, the Spaniards established missions and other settlements in *Baja* (meaning Lower) California. (This is the Mexican peninsula south of present-day California.)

Captain Gaspar de Portolá was made governor of Baja by the King of Spain. He led an expedition in 1769 that established the first *presidio* (military fort) at San Diego. He also established one at Monterey in 1770. Six years later, a group of Spanish settlers arrived where San Francisco is located today. It was known as *Yerba Buena* at that time.

Do these things using the map provided.

1. Trace over the broken line (– – – – – – – –) with a pen or pencil to show the route that Father Francisco Kino took across the Colorado River.

2. Write **New Spain** ①, **North America** ②, **Baja California** ③, **San Diego** ④, **Monterey** ⑤, **San Francisco** ⑥, **Atlantic Ocean** ⑦, **Pacific Ocean** ⑧ and **Gulf of Mexico** ⑨ by the correct number.

3. Color your map. Be neat!

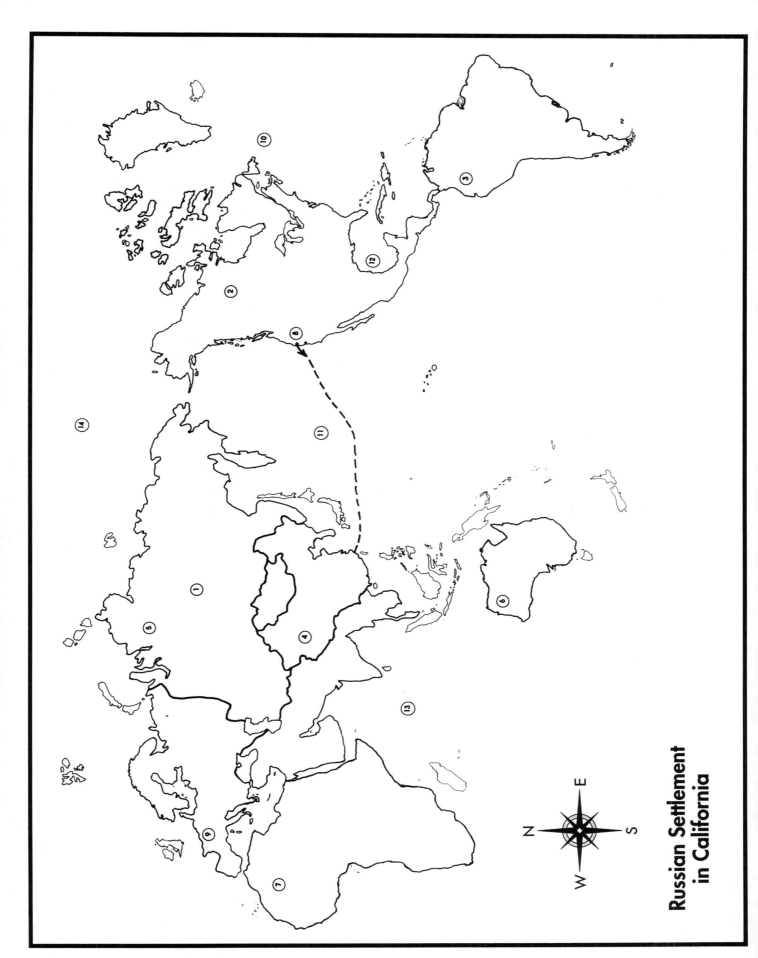

Russian Settlement
in California

California
Settlements

Name _____

Date _____

Russian

During the mid-1700's Russia had fur trading interests in Alaska. Russian trappers wanted to hunt for furs farther south along the Pacific Coast. In 1812, Russia established Fort Ross on the northern California coast, just north of Bodega Bay.

The Russian trappers caught and killed sea lions in the northern California waters. Beavers were also trapped. Then the trappers shipped the furs to China in exchange for Oriental goods, such as silk.

Russian activity in California was one reason for the **Monroe Doctrine** of 1823. (The *Monroe Doctrine* was written by the United States. It said that European countries could not set up any new colonies or territories in North and South America .) In 1824, Russia agreed to limit its settlements to Alaska. However, the Russians did not leave the California region until 1841.

Do these things using the map provided.

1. Trace over the broken line (– – – – – – – –) with a pen or pencil to show the route that the Russian trading ships took to China with their trapped furs.

2. Write **Russia** ①, **North America** ②, **South America** ③, **China** ④, **Asia** ⑤, **Australia** ⑥, **Africa** ⑦, **Fort Ross** ⑧, **Europe** ⑨, **Atlantic Ocean** ⑩, **Pacific Ocean** ⑪, **Gulf of Mexico** ⑫, **Indian Ocean** ⑬ and **Arctic Ocean** ⑭ by the correct number.

3. Color your map as neatly as you can. Use different colors for each continent and country.

☆☆ **Bonus Activity**
On another piece of paper, draw a picture of Fort Ross — the Russian settlement in northern California. You can draw it the way you think it might have looked or find a picture to copy.

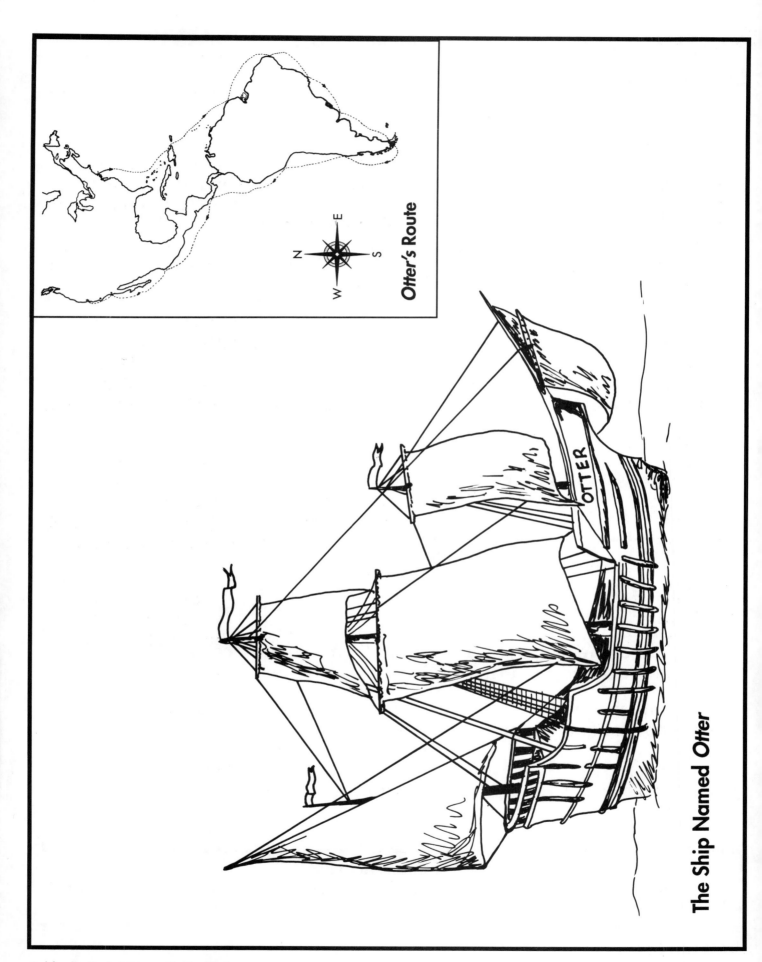

Otter's Route

The Ship Named Otter

California
Settlements

Name _____

Date _____

American

The *Otter* was the first American ship to reach the California coast from the East Coast, in 1796. It had to travel all the way around the southern tip of South America to get there. After the *Otter* came, many more trading ships came to the West Coast from the East Coast to trade goods. Sea otter and beaver furs were very popular on the East Coast to make into clothing. The Western territories had an **abundance** of the animals to trap, hunt, and then sell in the East.

Many settlers and traders were coming to California by ship. The first American to reach California by land was Jedediah Strong Smith. He was a trapper who crossed the southeastern deserts. Jedediah was called the *Bible Toter* because he had great faith in God and always carried a Bible. Other traders and explorers followed Jedediah by coming to California over the land.

Fifteen years after Jedediah's trip, the first **organized** group of American settlers came to California by land. They drove long wagon trains over the mountains and deserts, in all sorts of weather. It took several weeks to travel the long distance. The trips were very hard. Sometimes they ran out of food and had to hunt for it. They also ran out of water at times, and had to travel without any until they came to a river or lake. Sometimes babies were even born on the trip.

The new settlers did not like the way the Mexican government was ruling the **province**. They wanted California to become part of the United States. On a few different occasions, the United States offered to buy the land from Mexico, but Mexico would not sell it.

Do these things using the map provided.

1. Trace over the broken line (– – – – – – – –) with a pen or pencil to show the route that the American ship, the *Otter,* took to California.

2. Color the map and picture of the *Otter*.
   Do your best job coloring.
   You may even want to draw a simple picture on the ship's largest sail.

California Settlements

Name _____

Date _____

REVIEW QUESTIONS

Write the correct answer in the space provided.

1. Where is *Baja California*; and what does *Baja* mean? _____
_____

2. What did the maps of Father Eusebio Francisco Kino show about California?
_____

3. Explain which country wrote the *Monroe Doctrine* and briefly what it says.
_____
_____

4. Why did Russia build a fort in California? _____
_____

5. Describe the trips to California by wagon train. _____
_____
_____

6. What is a *presidio*?_____

7. Who established the first presidio in California?_____

Write the correct (best) answer on the line from the list of bold words.

Jesuit Priest _____

Gaspar de Portolá _____

Otter _____

Yerba Buena _____

California _____

King of Spain _____

Jedediah Smith _____

Bible Toter

Today's San Francisco

Ordered Settlements in California

1st American Ship to Reach Cal.

Governor of Baja California

Cartographer (Map Maker)

North America

Monterey

☆☆ Bonus Activity
Using another resource book, write a report on Jedediah Strong Smith, Jesuit priests, Eusebio Francisco Kino or the Monroe Doctrine. Make pictures to go along with your report.

New Words to Learn:

Find the words in a dictionary and write the meanings on the line.

1. **abuse:** _____

2. **adobe:** _____

3. **blacksmithing:** _____

4. **convert:** _____

5. **cruel:** _____

6. **discriminate:** _____

7. **empire:** _____

8. **Franciscan:** _____

9. **friar:** _____

10. **prosper:** _____

11. **province:** _____

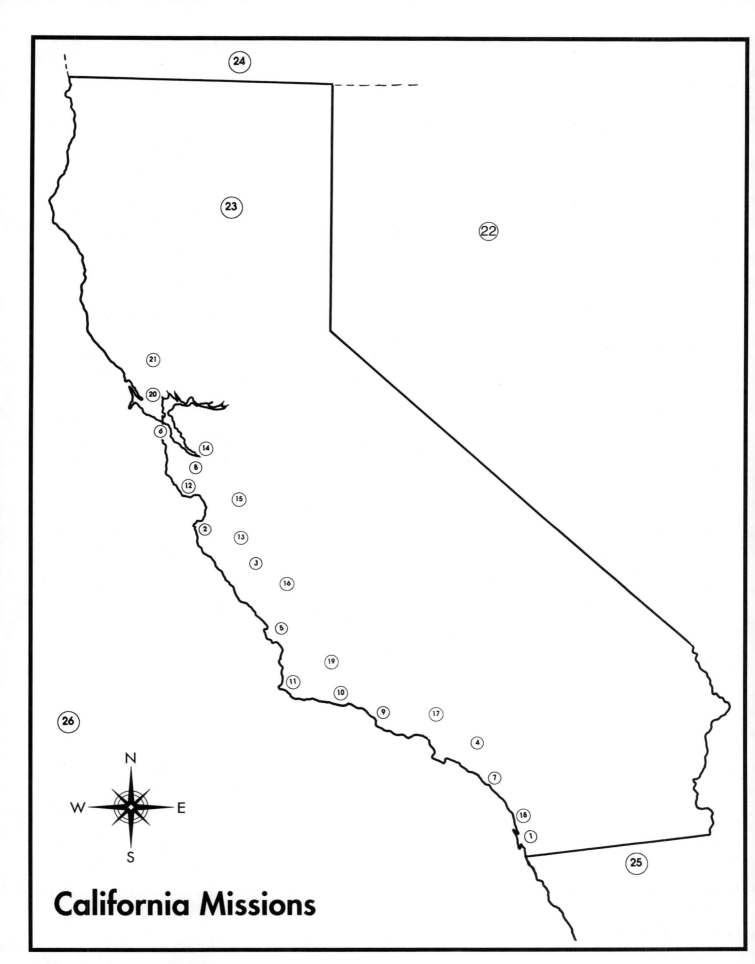

California Missions

California
Missions

Catholic Missions

The **Franciscan friars** of the Roman Catholic Church played a very important role in the Spanish settlement of California. During the 1769 expedition that Captain Gaspar de Portolá made to build the first *presidios* (military forts) at San Diego and Monterey, Father Junípero Serra established the first California mission.

The first missions of California were, in some ways, similar to today's churches. Even today, many churches send people to other countries to tell the people about God and their particular religion. These people are called *missionaries*. The California missions were established by the Catholic Church in order to **convert** the American Indians to the Catholic religion.

Father Serra began the first mission close to where San Diego is today. He named it *San Diego de Alcalá*. The last of the California missions was built near today's Sonoma, just north of San Francisco. It was named *San Francisco Solano* and built in 1823.

In the 54 years the Catholic Church was establishing itself in California, the Franciscans built a chain of 21 missions which "stretched" for a distance of over 525 miles. The missions were built about one day's horse ride from each other. This made it nice for travelers because they could have a place to sleep each night during their journey. The road the missions were built on was called *El Camino Real*, meaning The King's Highway.

Do these things using the map provided.

1. Write **Part of Mexico** ㉒, **California** ㉓, **Oregon Territory** ㉔, **Mexico** ㉕, and **Pacific Ocean** ㉖ by the correct number.

2. By the correct number, write the name of the town where the missions where built by the Franciscans. Write the year they where built as well.

San Diego -1769 ①	Santa Clara -1777 ⑧	San Juan Bautista-1797 ⑮
Carmel -1770 ②	Ventura -1782 ⑨	San Miguel-1797 ⑯
Jolon (San Antonio)-1771 ③	Santa Barbara -1786 ⑩	San Fernando-1797 ⑰
San Gabriel -1771 ④	Lompoc -1787 ⑪	San Luis Rey-1798 ⑱
San Luis Obispo -1772 ⑤	Santa Cruz -1791 ⑫	Solvang (Santa Ines) -1804 ⑲
San Francisco -1776 ⑥	Soledad -1791 ⑬	San Rafael-1817 ⑳
San Juan Capistrano -1776 ⑦	San Jose -1797 ⑭	Sonoma-1823 ㉑

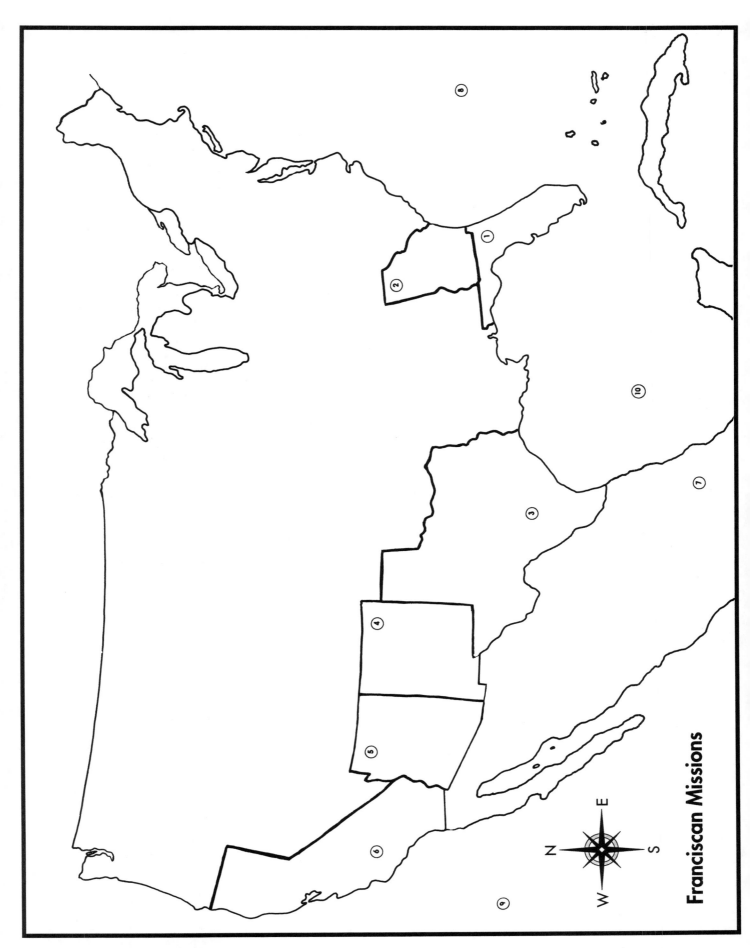

Franciscan Missions

California
Life on the Missions

Name _____

Date _____

American Missionary Life

Missionaries often led the way in establishing the first contact between white people and Native American people. The early Spanish missionaries arrived from Spain in the early 1500's. France and Great Britain (England) came in the 1600's. The main work of the French and British missions was to build frontier churches and schools. The Spanish missions, however, were actually small settlements or communities. The American Indians lived and worked at the Spanish missions, along with learning about the Catholic religion.

Members of the Franciscan order of the Roman Catholic Church founded most of the Spanish missions in what is now the United States. The missions spread across Spain's colonial **empire** of Mexico. The missions region included all or most of today's Florida, Georgia, Texas, New Mexico, Arizona and California.

The Spanish government supported and established the missions. It did so in order to develop new colonies and expand its empire. The government hoped the missionaries would convert the American Indians to the Catholic religion and teach them to become loyal to the Spanish government.

Do these things using the map provided.

1. Write the names of the states (or future states) where the Catholic Church established many missions:
   Florida ①, **Georgia** ②, **Texas** ③,
   New Mexico ④, **Arizona** ⑤ and **California** ⑥.
   Make sure they are by the correct number.

2. Write the names of the rest of the places on the map by the correct number:
   Mexico ⑦, **Atlantic Ocean** ⑧, **Pacific Ocean** ⑨
   and **Gulf of Mexico** ⑩.

3. Color your map. Be neat!

American Missionary Life Continued

The Spanish missions fed, clothed and often housed American Indians who came to them. In return, the Indians agreed to take lessons in Catholic religion, observe the Spanish customs and work on the mission.

Many missions included schools, storerooms, dining rooms, workshops and living quarters, as well as churches. Most of them were built out of stone blocks or **adobe** and also stood around a square courtyard. All of the missions had a farm and many operated cattle and horse ranches.

The Catholic religion was the main subject taught in the mission schools. Indian children attended religious classes at least twice a day. The missionaries also taught the children and adults how to read and write Spanish. They were also taught skills such as **blacksmithing**, candle making, leather-working, wine making and woodworking.

Most of the Indians living on the missions worked as farmers. They worked very hard on the farms. Some of them also became excellent ranchers and trade workers. The California Indians were highly productive. These missions developed good trade with ships from foreign countries to earn money and trade for goods. Some of the California missions grew into major agricultural (farming) and manufacturing centers.

Color this picture of a California mission.

American Missionary Life Continued

Activities on the missions followed a regular schedule. The day usually began with an early religious service. Breakfast was after the service and then the Indians went to work on their various jobs. They ate lunch at about noon and then went back to work for several more hours. After dinner they usually had time to themselves. However, at planting and harvest times, the Native Americans were forced to work several more hours each day and had little time for themselves or their families. Some Indians became ill from the long hours and died. Other Indians died from diseases brought to their homeland by Europeans.

Many Indians adjusted to daily life on the missions. However, many did not like the lack of their personal freedom. Large numbers of Indians left the missions. Spanish soldiers stationed near the missions often hunted and caught the Indians that fled and returned them to the missions.

Many of the white Spanish soldiers caused problems for the missionaries by **abusing** Indian women. The Indians often did not trust the missionaries, who were also white and Spanish, because of how **cruelly** the Spanish soldiers treated them. Some of the American Indians fought back against the white missionaries and soldiers by burning buildings and destroying crops. However, the soldiers had far better weapons and outnumbered the Indians. Because of this, the Indians could not change the way they were treated by the soldiers.

Color this picture of a different California mission.

Name _____

Date _____

Closing the Missions

In 1821, Mexico finally won its independence from Spanish rule. California became a **province** of the newly formed government in 1822. The new Mexican province set up its own government and established its own military force. The change in government did not hurt the missions at first. They continued to **prosper** until 1834.

Many people in both Mexico and California wanted to see the missions closed. In the early 1830's, the government began to sell mission land to private citizens. By 1846, almost all of the mission property had been sold.

Thousands of the American Indians who had been living on the missions when they closed faced several problems. Many of them did not want to return to tribal ways of life. However, **discrimination** and lack of education prevented even the highly skilled Indians from getting good jobs. They did not receive equal rights among the white people of the area. (Even today, Native Americans are "fighting" for equal rights among some white people, as well as other groups of people.)

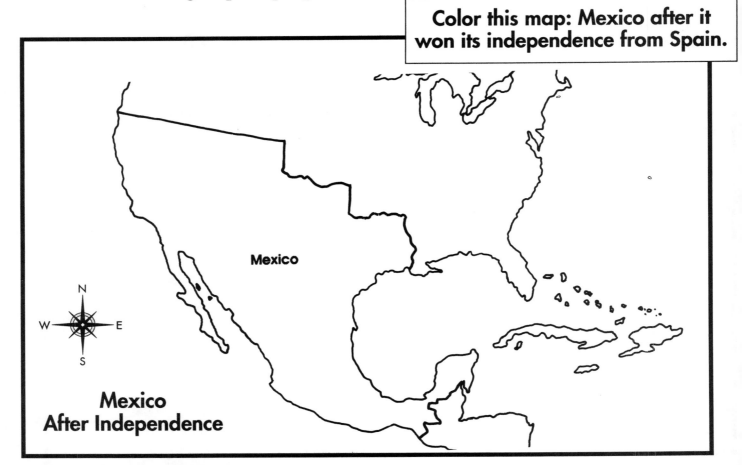

Color this map: Mexico after it won its independence from Spain.

N
W — E
S

Mexico

Mexico
After Independence

California
Missions

Write the correct answer in the space provided.

1. Describe, in detail, the part Franciscan friars had in the Spanish settlement of California. _____
_____
_____
_____
_____

2. Franciscan friars were part of which church (religion)? _____

3. How were Spanish missions different from the French or British Missions?
_____
_____
_____

4. Tell why the Spanish government helped establish Catholic missions.
_____
_____

5. Name at least five things that were taught to the Native Americans at the California missions. _____
_____

6. How do *you think* the Catholic Church decided where to build each mission?
_____
_____

7. Franciscans established missions in regions that were later to become which six states? _____
_____

8. Describe some of the problems that the Native Americans experienced when the missions closed. _____
_____
_____
_____

California
Missions

Name _____

Date _____

Write the correct answer in the space provided.

9. When the Spanish soldiers abused the Native American women, why did it cause problems for the missionaries?_____

_____

10. If you were one of the soldiers, what could you have done to help the Native American women? _____

_____

_____

Circle the best answer to each question.

11. During harvest time, the Native Americans on the missions had to work...

    a. long hours   b. short hours   c. only after breakfast

12. After Mexico won its independence from Spain, California became...

    a. New Spain   b. a province   c. a state   d. a territory

13. The main subject taught at the missions was...

    a. reading   b. writing   c. arithmetic   d. religion

14. The first mission in California was established near which present-day city?

    a. San Diego   b. Monterey   c. San Francisco   d. Baja

Write the correct answer to complete the sentences.

Father _____ established the first California mission during _____.
It was named _____ . The last California mission was built over
_____ miles north of the first one. It was named _____ . There
was a chain of _____ missions built along the road called _____ ,
which means the _____ . The year the last mission was built was _____ .

In the early 1830's, the _____ government began to _____ mission land
to _____ . By _____ , almost all of the mission _____ had been sold.

☆☆ **Bonus Activity**
Using another resource book, find a picture of a California mission. Draw pictures of your
own mission. Name it whatever you like. Write a list of things that you would have the
people living on your mission do for work and fun.

New Words to Learn:

Find the words in a dictionary and write the meanings on the line.

1. **admitted:** _____

2. **boundary:** _____

3. **cession:** _____

4. **manifest destiny:** _____

5. **occupy:** _____

6. **rebellion:** _____

7. **relation(s):** _____

8. **republic:** _____

9. **revolt:** _____

10. **survey:** _____

11. **treaty:** _____

Name _____

Date _____

Between 1844 and 1846, the military explorer John Frémont led two **surveying** parties into California. He was hired by the United States government to see what the land was like. The Mexican officials in California did not trust him or the American soldiers that were in his party. In March of 1846, his party was camped near the capital city of Monterey. At that time, the Mexican government ordered him to leave California.

Instead of leaving California, he went about 25 miles north of Monterey to *Hawk's Peak*. While there, he helped the American settlers who were upset with the Mexican government to organize a **revolt**. He began to build a fort there.

In June of 1846, without knowing that the United States had already declared war on Mexico, a group of American settlers took over the Mexican headquarters in Sonoma — General Vallejo's headquarters. The group was led by Ezekiel Merritt. After capturing the fort, the settlers raised their newly made flag over the fort. It had a white background, a grizzly bear standing on green grass in the middle, a red stripe along the bottom and red star near the top. The words, *California Republic,* were written on it. This event became known as the *Bear Flag Revolt*.

Color the flag of the *Bear Flag Revolt*.
Make sure you color it the way it is described in the above paragraph.

Mexican-American War

Name _____

Date _____

Background to the War

In 1835, Texas revolted against the Mexican government, which controlled the territory at that time. Texans won the revolt and established the Republic of Texas in 1836. However, Mexico refused to recognize Texas' independence. The Mexican government warned the United States that if Texas was **admitted** to the Union, Mexico would declare war on the United States. James Polk was elected President of the United States in 1844. He said he was in favor of Texas' becoming a state. In 1845, Texas did become a state. Mexico did not declare war, but broke off friendly **relations** with the United States.

Other arguments between the United States and Mexico developed. One of them was the question as to where the **boundary** was between Texas and Mexico. Texas claimed that the Rio Grande (Large River) would be its southwestern boundary. Mexico said that the Nueces River was to be the boundary.

Most important of all, was the feeling in the United States that the country had a **manifest destiny** to expand all the way to the Pacific Ocean. The movement westward had brought many Americans into Mexican territory, especially California. Mexico was too weak to control or populate these northern territories. Both Mexican and American settlers in California disliked the way in which Mexico was ruling the area.

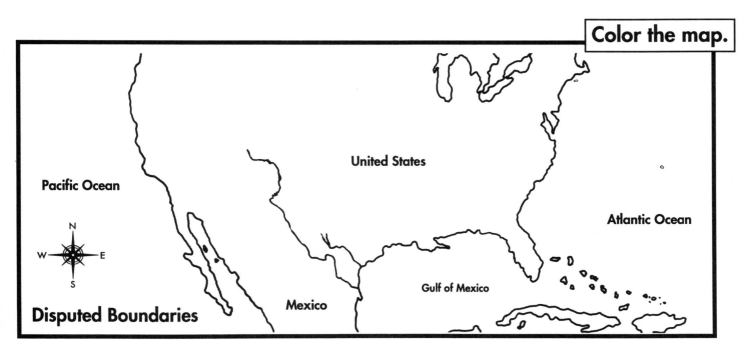

Color the map.

Pacific Ocean

United States

Atlantic Ocean

N
W   E
S

Gulf of Mexico

Mexico

Disputed Boundaries

Name _____

Date _____

Background to the War Continued

In the Fall of 1845, President Polk offered to pay Mexico 25 million dollars for the purchase of California and the Rio Grande border of Texas. Mexico refused the money. During this time, President Polk had ordered Army General Zachary Taylor and his men to go to the Rio Grande. On April 25th, a small group of American soldiers was attacked and defeated by a group of Mexican soldiers.

President Polk had already asked Congress to declare war on Mexico. The news of the battle allowed him to say that Mexico had, "invaded our territory and shed American blood on our soil." However, in reality, Mexico had as much right to claim the land in question as did the United States. It was not owned by the United States at that time. On May 13, 1846, the United States Congress declared war on Mexico.

The United States had two goals. They wanted to **occupy** the territory Mexico had refused to sell. They also wanted to invade Mexico in order to force the Mexicans to agree to peace.

Use this map for the activities at the bottom of page 51 of this section.

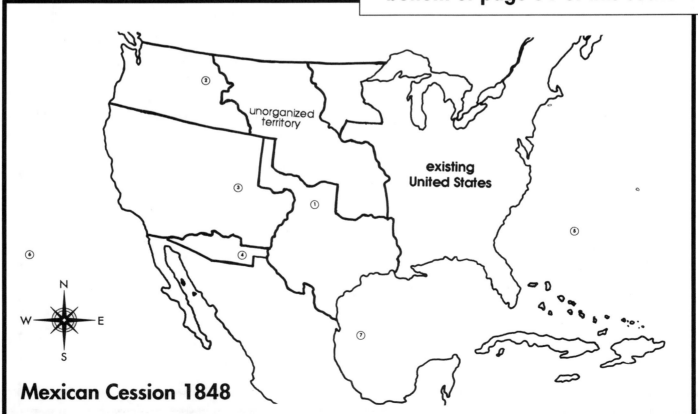

Mexican Cession 1848

California
Mexican-American War

Name _____

Date _____

Occupation of California

In June of 1846, General Stephen Kearny set out from Kansas with 1,700 men to capture New Mexico from the Mexican armies. In August, his troops went to the New Mexico town of Santa Fe and took control of the territory. In September, General Kearny and his men pushed across the desert and entered California territory.

Meanwhile, in June of 1846, a group of American settlers in Northern California began a **rebellion** against the Mexican government. This was the *Bear Flag Revolt*. In July, U.S. Naval forces, under the leadership of Commodore John Sloat, captured the capital town of Monterey. He and his sailors occupied the San Francisco area.

On December 6th, General Kearny led 100 soldiers in the bloody Battle of San Pasqual near San Diego. Reinforcements from San Diego had to be sent in to save the small American army from defeat.

In January of 1847, U.S. troops won the Battle of San Gabriel near Los Angeles. This gave the United States the victory they needed in order to gain control of California.

In 1819, a treaty between the United States and Spain fixed the present northern boundary of what was to become California. In 1846, a treaty with Great Britain fixed the northern boundary of the Oregon Territory shown on the map provided on page 50.

Do these things using the map provided.

(Use the map on page 50.)

1. Write **Texas Annexation 1845** ①,
   Oregon Territory Cession 1846 ②,
   Mexican Cession 1848 ③,
   Gadsden Purchase 1853 ④,
   Atlantic Ocean ⑤, **Pacific Ocean** ⑥
   and **Gulf of Mexico** ⑦
   by the correct number.

2. Do your best job when you color the map.
   Change colors for each of the different territories.

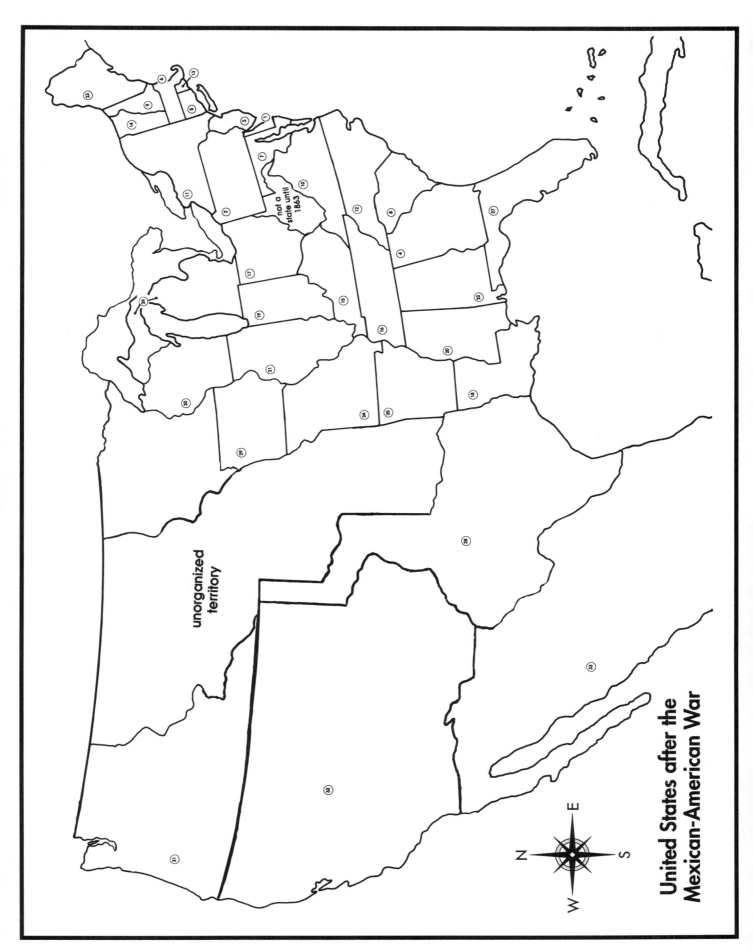

not a
state until
1863

unorganized
territory

United States after the
Mexican–American War

N
E
S
W

California
Mexican-American War

Name _____

Date _____

Results of the War

A **treaty** was signed by Mexico and the United States on February 2, 1848, at the village of Guadalupe Hidalgo, near Mexico City. It is called the *Treaty of Guadalupe Hidalgo*. By this time, many people in the United States wanted to take over the entire country of Mexico. However, the treaty required Mexico to give up only the territory President Polk originally asked for — to the Rio Grande, and California.

The United States paid Mexico 15 million dollars for the territories in what is known as the *Mexican Cession*. The **cession** covered what are now California, Nevada, Utah, part of Arizona, New Mexico, Colorado and Wyoming.

As the result of the Mexican-American War, the United States gained more than 525,000 square miles. It also brought the question to focus as to whether the new territory of California would support slavery or be a free state. The *Compromise of 1850* made California a free state. It also allowed the people of the territory the right to decide which way it would go, either free or slave.

Do these things using the map provided.

1. Write the names of the states and territories of the United States after the Mexican-American War ended. Make sure you write the name by the correct number. (Note that the states are ordered numerically according to the order they entered the United States.) *You will need to write small.*

Delaware ①	North Carolina ⑫	Maine ㉓
Pennsylvania ②	Rhode Island ⑬	Missouri ㉔
New Jersey ③	Vermont ⑭	Arkansas ㉕
Georgia ④	Kentucky ⑮	Michigan ㉖
Connecticut ⑤	Tennessee ⑯	Florida ㉗
Massachusetts ⑥	Ohio ⑰	Texas ㉘
Maryland ⑦	Louisiana ⑱	Iowa ㉙
South Carolina ⑧	Indiana ⑲	Wisconsin ㉚
New Hampshire ⑨	Mississippi ⑳	Oregon Territory ㉛
Virginia ⑩	Illinois ㉑	Mexican Cession ㉜
New York ⑪	Alabama ㉒	Mexico ㉝

California
Mexican-American War

Write the correct answer in the space provided.

1. Instead of leaving California like the Mexican government told him to, write where John Frémont went and what he did. _____
_____
_____

2. Describe the flag raised over Mexican headquarters in the *Bear Flag Revolt*.
_____
_____

3. Explain what the battle near Texas allowed President Polk to do.
_____
_____
_____

4. What did Mexico refuse to do when Texas won its independence? _____
_____

5. What was the warning Mexico gave to the United States after Texas had won its independence? _____
_____

6. What territory did the *Mexican Cession* give the United States?
_____
_____

7. What was the date and name of the battle that gave the United States control of California? _____

8. After the United States won the war, what important question was brought to focus about California? _____

9. Mexico was too weak to do what two things with its northern territories?
_____

10. What is the Rio Grande? _____

Circle the best answer to each question.

11. What year did Texas become a state?

      a. 1835   b. 1836   c. 1845   d. 1846   e 1848

12. The battle that gave the U.S. control of California was *near* the town of...

    a. Los Angeles   b. Monterey   c. Santa Fe   d. San Gabriel

13. What did the *Compromise of 1850* do?

    a. ended the Mexican-American War   b. gave Mexico $15 million

          c. made California a free state

14. What year did the Mexican-American War end?

      a. 1835   b. 1836   c. 1845   d. 1846   e 1848

15. Who was President of the United States during the Mexican-American War?

    a. James Polk   b. Ezekiel Merritt   c. John Frémont   d. Stephen Kearny

16. Who was the American who captured the town of Monterey?

    a. James Polk   b. Commodore Sloat c. John Frémont   d. Stephen Kearny

Write the correct (best) answer on the line from the list of bold words.

John Frémont _____

15 Million Dollars _____

Manifest Destiny _____

Ezekiel Merritt_____

Rio Grande_____

California Republic _____

Compromise of 1850_____

New Flag

U.S. Expansion to Pacific Ocean

Bear Flag Revolt Leader

Mexican Cession

Populate

Surveying Party

Free State

Mexico/Texas Border

☆☆ **Bonus Activities (Choose 1)**
Using another resource book, write a short report on on term *Manifest Destiny*.
Make a map and pictures of the United States during the Mexican-American War.

Notes & Doodles

New Words to Learn:

Find the words in a dictionary and write the meanings on the line.

1. **ancestry:**_____

2. **brochures:** _____

3. **exaggerate:** _____

4. **foreign:**_____

5. **image:** _____

6. **migrate:** _____

7. **respect** (disrespect): _____

8. **tedious:** _____

9. **transcontinental:** _____

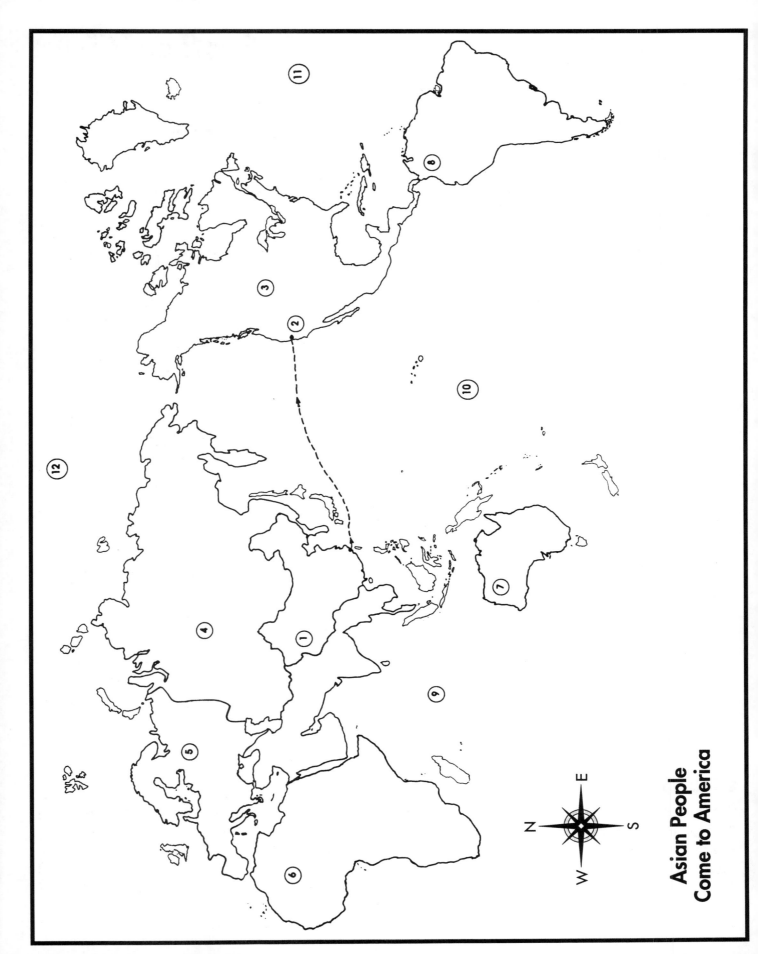

Asian People Come to America

California
Asian Americans

Early Chinese Migration

There are records of Chinese sailors and shipbuilders who reached the American continent as early as 1565. This paved the way for more Chinese people to **migrate** to America. There was a Chinese colony of people living in Mexico City as early as 1635.

However, the first large movement of Chinese people to come to America came around 1850, after the discovery of gold. Chinese prospectors came to find their fortunes in gold. They planned to return home to share their wealth with their families. Since they thought that they would be returning home after a short time in America, these early Chinese were usually men traveling alone. They did not bring their wives, children or other family members. However, most did not return to Asia as planned.

Because of the stories of gold, the Chinese called California and America *Gim Sahn*, or *Mountain of Gold*. They came in such large numbers that the Chinese were soon the largest group of California prospectors born in a **foreign** country.

Do these things using the map provided.

1. Trace over the broken line (– – – – – – – –) with a pen or pencil to show the route that Chinese people took to California.

2. Write **China** ①, **San Francisco** ②,
   North America ③, **Asia** ④,
   Europe ⑤, **Africa** ⑥, **Australia** ⑦,
   South America ⑧, **Indian Ocean** ⑨,
   Pacific Ocean ⑩, **Atlantic Ocean** ⑪,
   and **Arctic Ocean** ⑫ by the correct number.

3. Color your map as nicely as you can.
   Color each continent a different color.

Note: Except for *very* rare exceptions the Japanese and people from other Asian countries came to California several years after the Gold Rush of 1848. One reason being, that until 1866, it was against the law for a "common" person to leave Japan. There were only about 86 Japanese people living in California by 1880. However, the Japanese and other Asian people have had a definite contribution to California's growth since statehood.

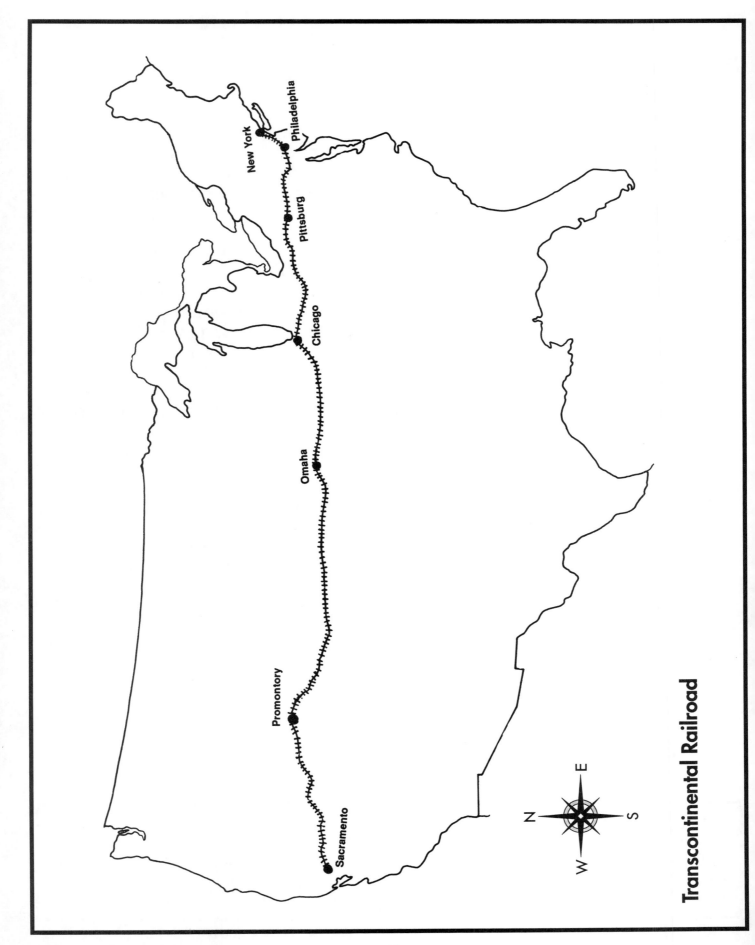

Philadelphia

New York

Pittsburg

Chicago

Omaha

Promontory

Sacramento

N E S W

Transcontinental Railroad

California
Asian Americans

Name _____

Date _____

Building Railroads

The discovery of gold in California in 1848 sparked trade by ship owners. They wanted Chinese passengers to travel to the United States. Printed **brochures exaggerated** the amount of gold to be found in California. The brochures suggested that gold was just lying in the middle of the street in America, just waiting to be picked up. When Asian people arrived in America, the truth was that there was only limited gold mining and other jobs.

The white population controlled the job market as well as making the laws. The jobs that the Asian workers usually got were the ones that other workers did not want. Some of the jobs were hard, **tedious** and low paying, such as harvesting crops and factory work. Other jobs were dangerous, like building tunnels and railroads. Some jobs, like cooking, cleaning and doing laundry were considered "women's work." The Asian people did these types of jobs in order to send money to their families in China, even though they suffered **disrespect**.

The Chinese people provided 95% of the workers who built the western half of the **Transcontinental Railroad**. They were hired by the Central Pacific Railroad to build the railroad eastward from Sacramento. They would be met by the Union Pacific workers who started laying track westward from Omaha, Nebraska.

Do these things using the map provided.

1. Color the track from Sacramento to Promontory gold or orange. (This is the track that the Chinese people built, working for the Central Pacific.)

2. Color the track from Omaha to Promontory blue or purple. (This is the track that the Union Pacific Railroad built.)

3. Very lightly, color the rest of the country one of your favorite colors.

Note: Before the 1960's, the term *Oriental* was often used to refer to people from Asia. The term *Asian American* was created by the Asian people themselves. This shows their own choice of a common name, rather than one given to them by the white Americans of the gold rush days.

However, some Asian people today still prefer the term *Oriental*. Many of them feel that they will be treated badly by non-Asians if they try to change their **image** and select a new name. These people have usually suffered **discrimination** and hardships in the past, just because they were of Asian **ancestry**. Because of their fear of more hardships, they choose to not challenge the term Oriental.

California
Asian Americans

REVIEW QUESTIONS

Write the correct answer in the space provided.

1. When did the first large movement of Asian people come to America, and why did they come?_____
_____
_____

2. What was the *picture* of America given by the stories of gold? _____
_____

3. Explain why ship owners printed the lies about the gold being found in America._____
_____

4. Why did the Asian men coming to America *not* bring their families?
_____
_____

5. Why could the Asian workers only get the jobs nobody else wanted?
_____
_____

6. In your own words, write the meaning of *discrimination*. _____
_____
_____

Circle the best answer to each question.

7. Many of the jobs Asian people were forced to take were considered…

    a. respectful   b. golden   c. women's work

8. Asian men first traveled to America to find their…

    a. fortunes   b. new family   c. brothers

☆☆ **Bonus Activity (Choose 1)**
Using another resource book, write a report on some aspect about China — either
past or present. Make pictures to go with your report.
Interview one or more persons with Asian ancestry.
Try to get information about them, their parents, and their grandparents.

California Early History
Gold Rush of 1848

New Words to Learn:

Find the words in a dictionary and write the meanings on the line.

1. **abandon:**_____

2. **cape** (the land form):_____

3. **flock(ed):**_____

4. **fortune:**_____

5. (land) **grant:**_____

6. **harbor:**_____

7. **isthmus:**_____

8. **pioneer:**_____

9. **seek(er):**_____

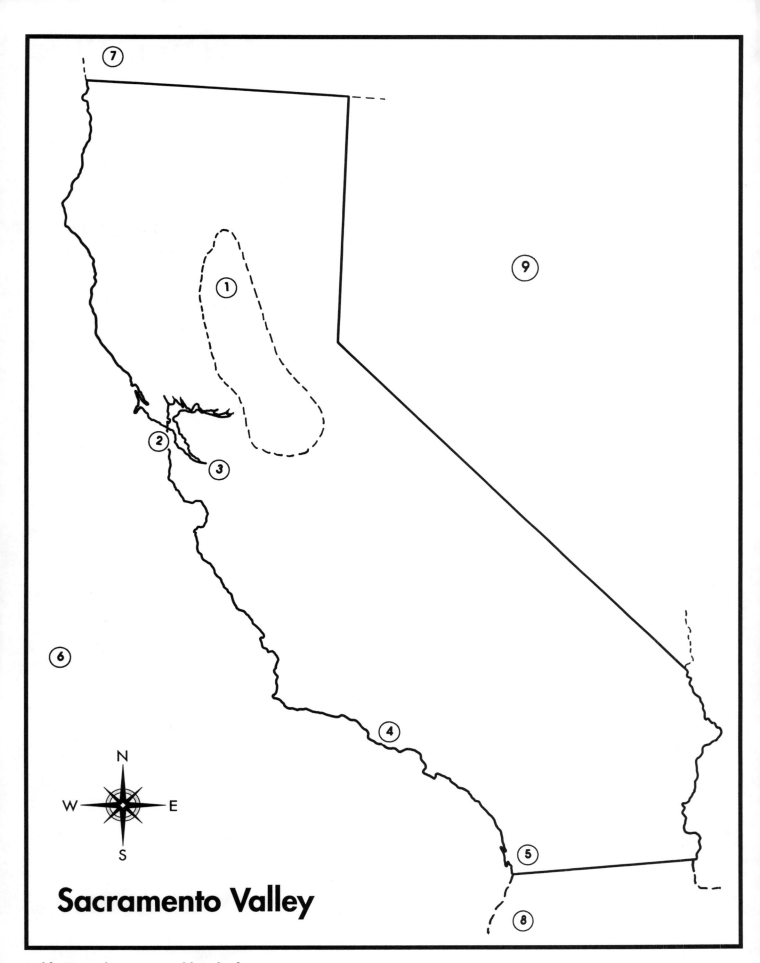

Sacramento Valley

California
Gold Rush of 1848

Name _____

Date _____

Gold Discovered

Just before the United States and Mexico signed the *Treaty of Guadalupe Hidalgo,* ending the Mexican-American War, gold was discovered in California. A **pioneer** trader named John A. Sutter had received a large land **grant** in the Sacramento Valley in 1839. Sutter had hired a carpenter named James W. Marshall (J. Sutter called him John) to build a sawmill on the American River.

While working on the sawmill on January 24, 1848, James Marshall found a piece of shiny metal about half the size of a pea. When he pounded it with a hammer he found that it was soft. Then he knew for sure he had discovered gold.

News of the gold discovery spread very quickly. Within one year the news of the gold found in California had spread around the world.

Do these things using the map provided.

1. Trace over the broken line (– – – – – – – –) with a pen or pencil to show the Sacramento Valley where gold was first discovered.

2. Write **Sacramento Valley** ①, **San Francisco** ②, **San Jose** ③, **Los Angeles** ④, **San Diego** ⑤, **Pacific Ocean** ⑥, **Oregon Territory** ⑦, **Mexico** ⑧ and **Nevada** ⑨ by the correct number.

3. Color your map as neatly as you can. Make the Sacramento Valley gold or orange and the rest of California any color you like.

☆☆ Bonus Activity
On another piece of paper, draw a picture of how you think John Sutter's saw mill looked.

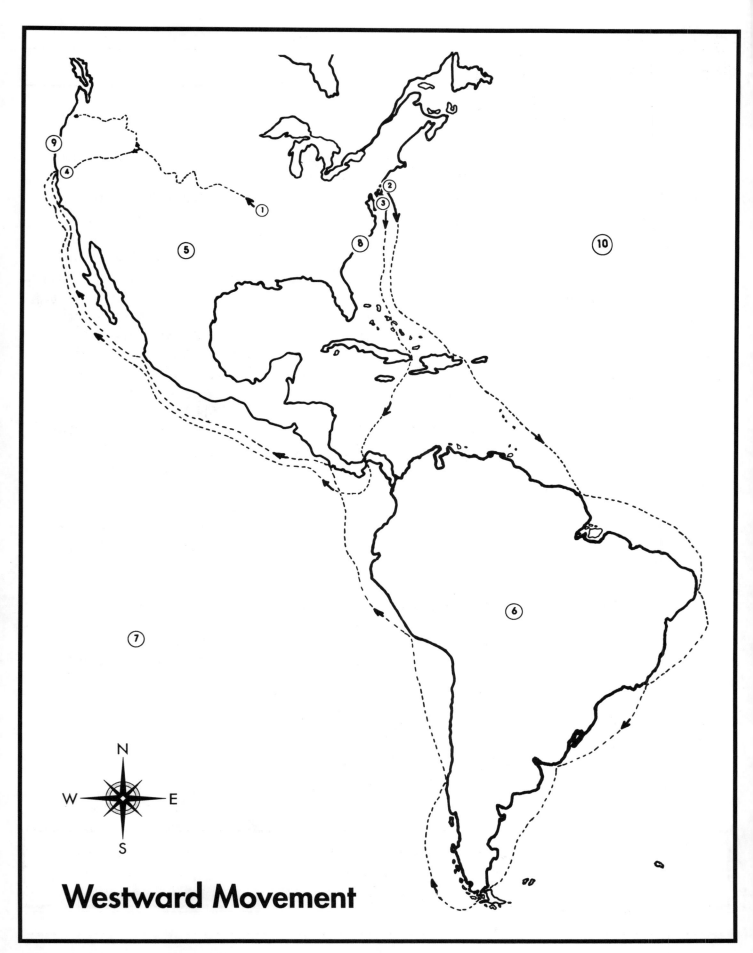

Westward Movement

California
Gold Rush of 1848

Name _____

Date _____

Westward Movement

In addition to the many Asian people coming to California, people came from all over the United States to find their fortune in gold. These **fortune-seekers** were called *forty-niners*, because it was 1849 when the large numbers of people **flocked** to the San Francisco area.

The first forty-niners to reach San Francisco arrived on February 28, 1849. They came on the ship named *California*. Other ships from all over the world came to the area carrying gold-seekers.

There were three main routes that the forty-niners took to reach the West Coast from the East Coast. One of the routes was to sail around the southern tip of South America. This "tip" is named **Cape Horn**, and the route was called the *Cape Horn Route*.

A shorter route was through Central America. The ships would carry the travelers to *Nicaragua* or the **Isthmus of Panama**. From there, the forty-niners crossed the country over the land to the Pacific Ocean. Then they would board another ship that would carry them to the San Francisco area.

However, the greatest number of people arrived from the Eastern states by covered wagon trains. They usually traveled over the *Oregon Trail,* as it was the safest route. Entire families moved to the area.

Do these things using the map provided.

1. Trace over the broken line (– – – – – – – –) with a pen or pencil to show the three routes to California during the *Westward Movement.*

2. Write **Oregon Trail** ①, **Cape Horn Route** ②,
   Panama Route ③, **San Francisco** ④,
   North America ⑤, **South America** ⑥,
   Pacific Ocean ⑦, **East Coast** ⑧,
   West Coast ⑨ and **Atlantic Ocean** ⑩
   by the correct number.

Note: Up until the time Mexico lost California to the United States in the Mexican-American War, *all* private land was owned by Mexican people. However, after the war and the overrunning of the land during the gold rush, the Mexican land owners rapidly lost their land to white settlers.

California
Gold Rush of 1848

Name _____

Date _____

Westward Movement Continued

San Francisco

Hundreds of ships jammed into the San Francisco **harbor** during 1849. They brought thousands of gold-seekers to the area. Many of the gold-hungry crews **abandoned** their ships in the harbor in order to search for gold. San Francisco became the supply center for the entire gold rush.

By the end of 1849, California's population increased from only 20,000 to over 107,000. In twelve years, from 1848 to 1860, California's population soared from 20,000 to almost 380,000 people. San Francisco grew from a small town of about 800 people to a large city of over 25,000 people by 1850.

In addition to the population of San Francisco soaring, the price of living in the city also soared. There was so much gold in the area and not enough products to support the rise in population. Prices of food, clothing and housing went "sky-high." Small shacks rented for over $100 per week. Food prices rose 10-15 times the normal price. The people who had lived there before the discovery of gold and the ones who did not find gold had a very hard time affording to live in the area because of the higher prices. (This type of rising prices is known as *inflation*.)

Color the picture of these California prospectors.

California
Gold Rush of 1848

REVIEW QUESTIONS

Write the correct answer in the space provided.

1. Tell what the term *forty-niner* meant during the California gold rush.

_____

2. Describe two of the three main routes the forty-niners took to get
to California. (a.) _____

_____

(b.) _____

_____

3. Where was James Marshall when he discovered gold? _____

_____

4. Explain why many of the people who did not find gold had a hard time
paying for food, rent and other things._____

_____

Write the correct answer to complete the sentences.

In _____ , James Marshall found _____ at _____ sawmill. The
sawmill was located in the _____ . Within one _____ the
news had traveled _____ .

The first forty-niners arrived on the ship named _____ . The date
was _____ . _____ of the ships came to the
San Francisco harbor during 1849. Many of the _____ crews
_____ their ships in order to search for _____ .

California's _____ increased from _____ to
over _____ in one year. San Francisco grew from a_____
_____ to a _____ of over 25,000 _____ by _____ .

```
☆☆ Bonus Activities
Write a story pretending you were a Forty-Niner (not a football player).  Tell where you
moved from, your ethnic heritage, how you reached California and if you found gold.
If you did find gold, tell how it changed your life and what you did with the gold.
Make pictures and maps to go along with your story.
```

NOTES & DOODLES

California
Early History

Statehood & Symbols

Use this as your "Read Aloud" copy.
Definitions listed

New Words to Le...

Find the words in a ... he line.

1. **capital:** City ... re govt is based

2. **capitol:** Th ... nakers meet

3. **commercial** ... making money

4. **Congress:** t ... he U.S.

5. **constitution:** basic laws of a country that states the rights of its people and the power of the govt.

6. **convention:** formal gathering of people who have the same interests

7. **debate:** discussion where people different opinions

8. **determination:** a strong intention to do something

9. **governor:** _____

10. **symbol:** a design or object that stands or represents something else.

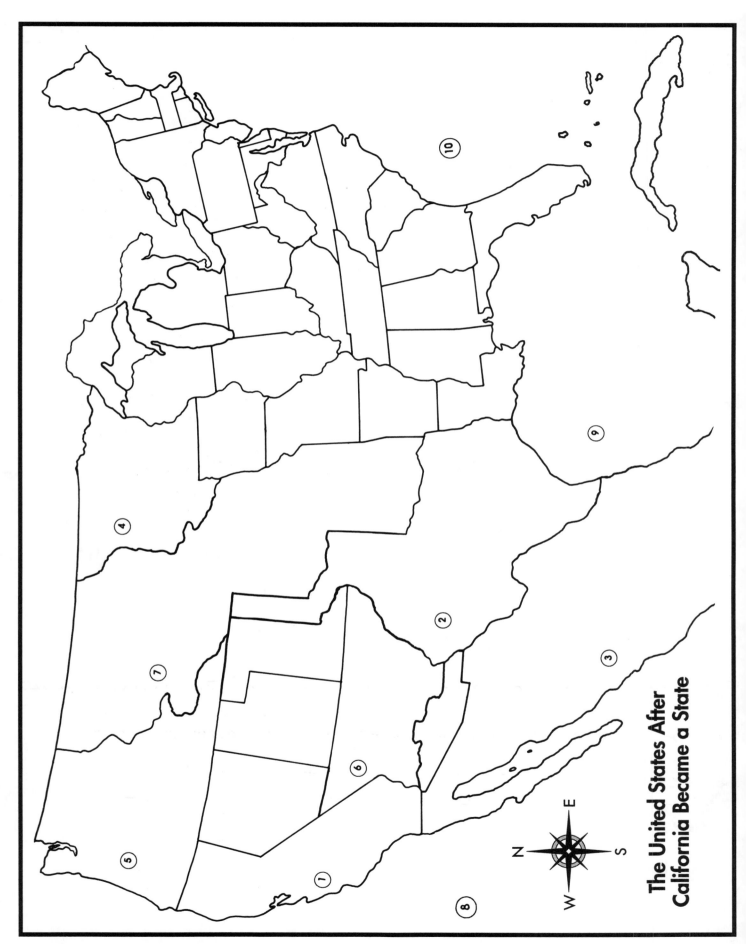

The United States After California Became a State

California
Statehood
September 9, 1850 — 31st State of the Union

During the westward movement, California was only a territory owned by the United States. As a territory, the people of the area did not have a voice in the **government** of the United States. They had to do whatever the U.S. government said, and had no input into what they decided. As a state, they could form their own government and vote for themselves on many state laws.

During 1849, local people in the **capital** city of Monterey organized a **Constitutional Convention**. They wanted to form a state government. The people voted on and accepted a **constitution** for the state.

The United States **Congress**, however, did not accept California as a state. The population increased greatly with the forty-niners coming to California. This increase in population helped the territory to become a state because there were so many more people living in the territory that Congress listened to their wishes. After a long **debate**, Congress finally admitted California to the Union of the United States. On September 9, 1850, California was the 31st state admitted to the Union.

Do these things using the map provided.

1. Write **California** (1), **Texas** (2), **Mexico** (3),
   Minnesota Territory (4), **Oregon Territory** (5),
   New Mexico Territory (6), **Unorganized Territory** (7),
   Pacific Ocean (8), **Gulf of Mexico** (9) and **Atlantic Ocean** (10)
   by the correct number.

☆☆ Bonus Activity
Using another resource, write the names of the rest of the states that are drawn on the map.
You could also use the map you completed on page 52, Section 7.
You need to complete this before you color the map.

---

2. Color California gold or orange. Use any other colors for the rest of
   your map. Change colors for each of the territories on the map.

California
Statehood
September 9, 1850 — 31st State of the Union

State Seal

The State Seal was adopted a year before California was admitted to the Union. The grizzly bear on the seal is the **symbol** of **determination**. The bear stands near the Roman goddess of wisdom. The miner in the background represents the state's mining industry. The ships in the harbor symbolize **commercial** greatness. The peaks in the background are the Sierra Nevada Mountains. The thirty-one stars show that California was the thirty-first state.

Color the California State Seal.
(The real seal is gold colored, but
  you can pick your own color.)

California
Statehood
September 9, 1850 — 31st State of the Union

Name _____

Date _____

Capital

Between 1850 and 1854, San Jose, Vallejo and San Francisco served as the temporary capital cities. In 1854, the capital city was permanently moved to Sacramento. The dome on the capitol rises 247 feet above the ground.

The first **Governor** of California was Peter H. Burnett. It took several years to complete the construction of the **Governor's Mansion**. It was first occupied in 1869.

Color this picture of California's Capitol building.

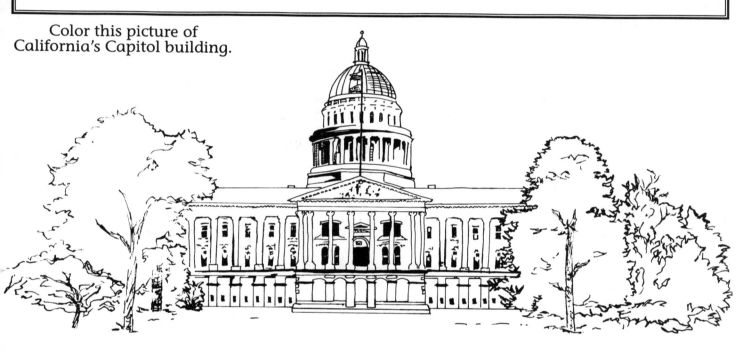

State Flag

The state flag was officially adopted in 1911. However, it was first designed and raised in 1846. It was raised above the Mexican head-quarters in Sonoma during the *"Bear Flag Revolt."* Americans raised it who were rebelling against Mexican rule. Today's flag looks very much like the one raised in the revolt. The star and stripe are both red. The background is white and the bear is standing on green grass.

CALIFORNIA REPUBLIC

Color the California Flag.

California
State Symbols
Statehood September 9, 1850 — 31st State

Name _____

Date _____

Color the pictures.

State Mineral
Gold

State Insect
Dog Face Butterfly

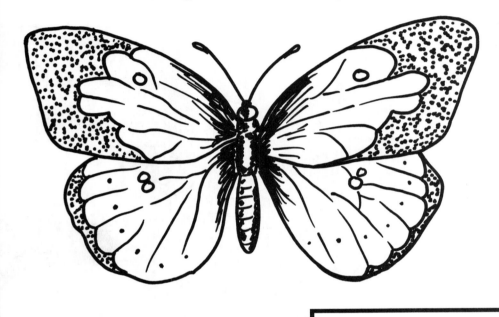

State Reptile
Desert Tortoise

State Nickname
"The Golden State"

California
State Symbols
Statehood September 9, 1850 — 31st State

Color the pictures.

State Tree
California Redwood

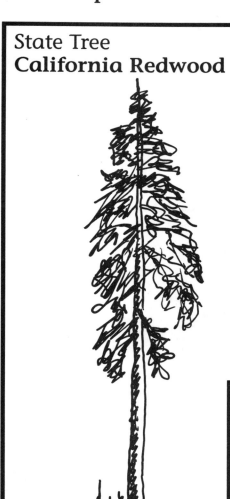

State Song

"I Love You, California"

words by F.B. Silverwood;
music by A. F. Frankenstein

State Animal
Grizzly Bear

State Flower
Golden Poppy

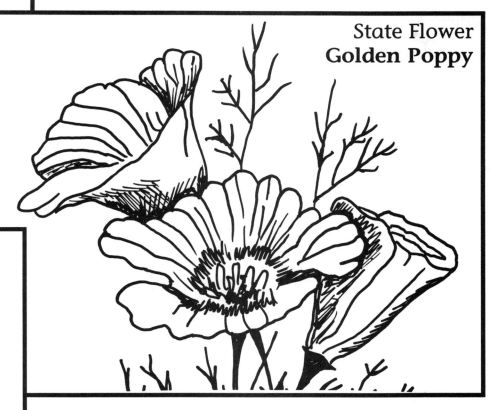

California
State Symbols
Statehood September 9, 1850 — 31st State

Color the pictures.

State Bird
California Valley Quail

State Rock
Serpentine

State Marine Mammal
California Gray Whale

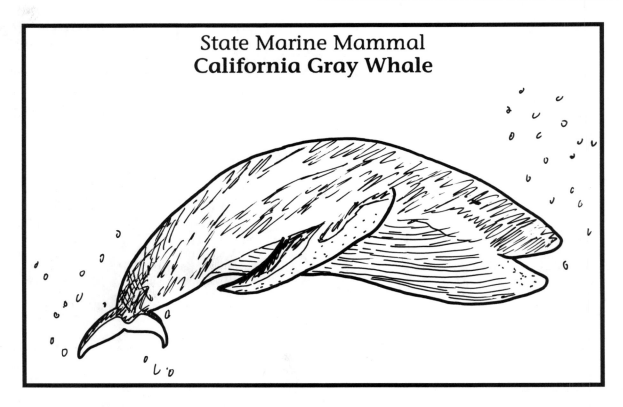

State Motto
"Eureka"
I have found it!

California
State Symbols
Statehood September 9, 1850 — 31st State

Name _____

Date _____

Color the pictures.

State Fish
Golden Trout

California is...

...the 3rd largest state in area.

...the largest state in population (about 32 million people).

California has...

...the largest population of Native Americans than any other state.

...one of the largest Chinese communities outside Asia in the entire world (San Francisco).

California is...

...the largest producer of goods of all the states and the largest agricultural state in the Union.

Largest City
Los Angeles
(the 2nd largest city in the U.S.)

The Los Angeles area has more people of Mexican ancestry than any other urban area (city) in the world, outside of Mexico.

State Fossil
Saber-Toothed Cat

Highest Mountain
Mt. Whitney
(14, 494 ft. above sea level)

Lowest Elevation
Death Valley
(282 ft. below sea level)

California
Statehood & Symbols

REVIEW QUESTIONS

Write the correct answer in the space provided.

1. Why did the people of California want to become a state? _____

_____

_____

2. Who was the first Governor of California? _____

3. Describe what the first California flag looked like. _____

4. What helped the United States Congress to allow California to become a state?

_____

_____

_____

Write the correct (best) answer on the line from the list of bold words.

September 9, 1850_____   **California**

State Animal_____   **Gold**

State Bird _____   **Golden State**

Sacramento_____   **Golden Poppy**

State Tree _____   **California Statehood**

State Mineral _____   **Valley Quail**

State Insect _____   **First State Capital**

Nickname _____   **Permanent State Capital**

State Flower_____   **Gray Whale**

Monterey _____   **Redwood**

Thirty-First State _____   **Grizzly Bear**

State Marine Mammal_____   **Dog Face Butterfly**

☆☆ Bonus Activity
Using another resource book, write a report on one or more of any of California's
state symbols, animals, etc. Include pictures in your report.

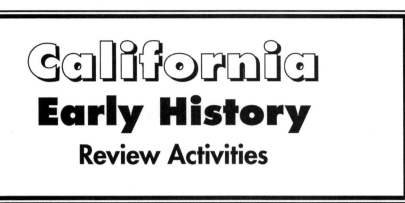

California
Early History
Review Activities

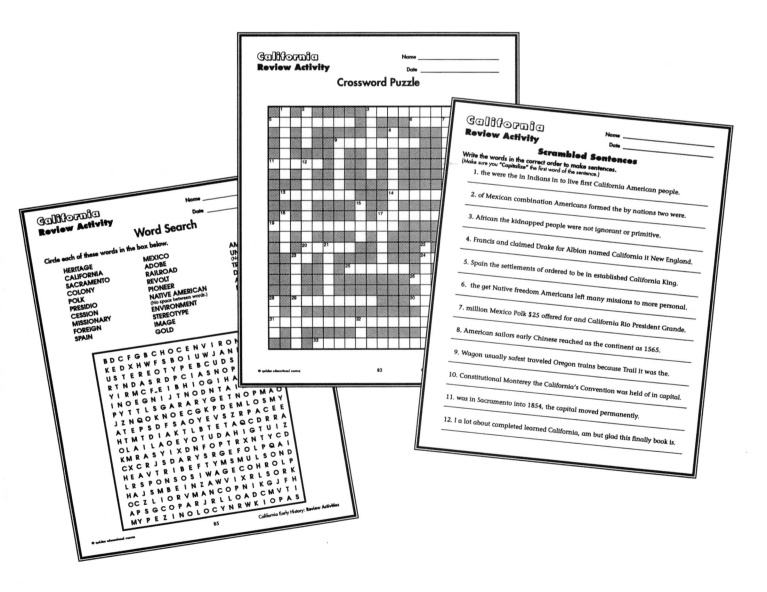

Crossword Puzzle

Across

3. This happened on September 9, 1850.
5. Today's Mexico was first named this by a European country.
6. He urged the King of Spain to establish colonies in California.
9. The first capital of California.
11. A highly developed civilization, located where Mexico is today.
13. Indentured servants in the United States could work and earn this.
14. Father Kino crossed the Colorado River and went into this region.
17. To travel from one place to another. (Like the forty-niners, & Asian men.)
19. A person who makes maps. (Father Kino was good at it.)
20. The name of the first American ship to reach the California coast from the East.
24. One of the men at Fort Ross (just north of Bodega Bay.)
25. He owned a sawmill in the Sacramento Valley.
26. Sir Francis Drake explored California and sailed _____ the world.
29. Asian men were responsible for building most of this.
30. The dividing line between any states or countries is called this.
31. The feeling in the United States about expanding to the Pacific Ocean.
33. Nickname of California.

Down

1. A child with a Spanish and an Indian parent.
2. The Chinese prospectors came from this continent.
3. General Kearny stopped here before he went into California.
4. These brought most of the people West.
7. Probably the first European to see the coast of California.
8. A person who searches for gold or other valuable ore.
9. California was a province of this country.
10. The King of Spain was urged to do this with California.
12. Explorers often took one of these missions.
15. These Native Americans lived in the northwestern region of California.
16. A Spanish word, meaning *lower*.
17. Father Eusebio Francisco Kino was a member of this Catholic *order*.
18. This was the first name of the area known as San Francisco.
21. Native Americans saw themselves as this type of person, not *Indian*.
22. If you think all of one group of people are the same you do this.
23. The United States wanted this as the southern boundary of Texas.
27. Slave trade was introduced in the Americas because it would produce a lot of this.
28. These American Indians lived in the southern region of California.
32. Long working hours and European diseases caused many Indians to do this on the California missions.

Crossword Puzzle

Scrambled Sentences

Write the words in the correct order to make sentences.
(Make sure you *capitalize* the first word of the sentence.)

1. the were the Native in to live first California Americans people.

   _____

2. of Mexican combination Americans formed the by nations two were.

   _____

3. people African the ignorant kidnapped were not or primitive.

   _____

4. Francis and claimed Drake for Albion named California it New England.

   _____

5. Spain the settlements of ordered to be in established California King.

   _____

6. the get Native freedom Americans left many missions to more personal.

   _____

7. million Mexico Polk $25 offered for and California Rio President Grande.

   _____

8. American sailors early Chinese reached as the continent as 1565.

   _____

9. Wagon usually safest traveled Oregon trains because Trail it was the.

   _____

10. Constitutional Monterey the California's Convention was held of in capital.

    _____

11. was in Sacramento to 1854, the capital moved permanently.

    _____

12. I a lot about completed learned California, am but glad this finally book is.

    _____

California
Review Activity

Word Search

Circle each of these words in the box below.

HERITAGE	MEXICO	AMERICA
CALIFORNIA	ADOBE	UNITED STATES
SACRAMENTO	RAILROAD	(No space between words.)
COLONY	REVOLT	TREATY
POLK	PIONEER	DESTINY
PRESIDIO	NATIVE AMERICAN	AZTEC
CESSION	(No space between words.)	ROUTE
MISSIONARY	ENVIRONMENT	COLONIZE
FOREIGN	STEREOTYPE	TRIBE
SPAIN	IMAGE	CULTURE
	GOLD	

```
B D C F G B C H O C E N V I R O N M E N T
K E D X H W F S B O I U W J A N B V N A L
U S T E R E O T Y P E B C U D S P M T T O
R T N D A S R D P C I A S N O P T S G I V
Y I R M C F E I B H I O G I H A L F W V E
I N O E G N I J T N O D N T A I M A G E R
P Y T T L S G A R A R Y G E T N O P M A O
J Z N Q O K N O E C G K P D E M L O S M Y
A T E P S D F S A O Y E V S Z R P A C E E
H T M T D I A K T L B T E T A Q C D R R A
O L A I L A O E Y O T U D A H I G T U I Z
K M R A S Y I X D N F O P T R X N T Y C D
C X C R J S D A R Y S R G E F O L P Q A I
H E A V T R I B E F T Y M S M U L S O N D
L R S P O N S O S I W A G E C O H R O L P
H A J S M B E I N Z A W V I X R L S O R K
O C Z L I O R V M A N C O P N I K G J F H
A P S G C O P A R J R L L O A D C M V T I
M Y P E Z I N O L O C Y N R W K I O P A S
```

Notes & Doodles

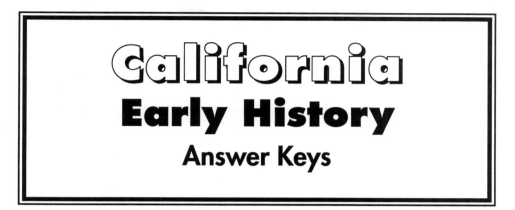

California Early History
Answer Keys

Suggestions for using these answer keys:

Answer keys have been provided for each of the sections in this book. We suggest that answer keys be made available to your students in order for them to correct their own work. If your students can use the answer keys provided in this section, duplicate and laminate them and allow them to check their own work (except for the answers that need to be checked by a teacher).

If your students are unable to use the answer sheets provided, duplicate each of the review questions and review activities. Complete them with a colored pen that is easily distinguished from the questions — red, orange or green work well. We also suggest that you laminate these pages and place them in a 3-ring binder to keep them organized and clean. This will also allow them to last much longer.

Section 1 – page 10
1. All Indians are alike.
2. People crossed from Asia to N. America by land near the Bering Sea.
3. Columbus thought he landed in India.
4. gathering
5. b. its environment
6. c. 200
7. a. lived off the land

Hupa – **northwestern**
Míwok – **north of San Francisco**
Maidu – **central**
Pomo – **north of San Francisco**
Modoc – **northern border**
Mohave – **southeastern**
Yuma – **southeastern**

Section 3 – page 22
1. Africa is SE of N. America. It is the shortest ship route.
2. It produced huge profits for European Businessmen
3. You could work off a debt by serving the lender for a period of years.
4. They were kidnapped into slavery.
5. *Teacher check*

Sold into Slavery – **African People**
First Black Explorer – **Diego el Negro**
Indentured Servants – **worked for their freedom**
Organized Civilizations – **10 million African people**
New England – **earliest Black settlers**

Section 5 – page 36
1. South of California – "lower"
2. California was a part of North America.
3. the U.S.;European countries could not set up new colonies in territories in North & South America.
4. They wanted to hunt for furs in California.
5. *Teacher Check*
6. military fort
7. Gaspar de Portolá

Jesuit Priest – **cartographer (mapmaker)**
Gaspar de Portolá – **Governor of Baja California**
Otter – **first American ship reaching California**
Yerba Buena – **today's San Francisco**
California – **North America**
King of Spain – **ordered settlements in California**

Section 2 – page 16
1. *Teacher Check*
2. They have been formed by two different cultures and nations.
3. wealth and beauty
4. They destroyed the Aztecs and took their gold and land.
5. a person with Spanish and Native American parents
6. *Teacher Check*
7. c. New Spain
8. a. Mexico City
9. c. Gold

Section 4 – page 28
1. New Spain
2. *Teacher Check*
3. He died from an infection from a broken arm or leg.
4. San Diego Bay
5. a waterway to Asia and a city of gold
6. around the world
7. c. England
8. b. Juan Cabrillo
9. a. Sebastían Vizcaíno
10. b. Spain

Section 6 (page 1 of 2) – page 45
1. *Teacher Check*
2. Roman Catholic
3. Spanish missions were small settlements. French and British missions just built schools & churches.
4. develop new colonies to expand its empire
5. read & write Spanish, Catholic religion, candle making, blacksmithing, leather-working, wine making, woodworking.
6. *Teacher Check*
7. California, Arizona, New Mexico, Texas, Georgia and Florida
8. No good jobs & no equal rights among whites.

California
Early History

Section 6 (page 2 of 2) – page 46

9. Indians would not trust the white/Spanish missionaries because the soldiers were white & Spanish.
10. *Teacher Check*
11. a. long hours
12. b. province
13. d. religion
14. a. San Diego

Junípero Serra; 1769; San Diego de Alcalá; 525; San Francisco Solano; 21; El Camino Real; The King's Highway; 1823; Mexican; sell; private citizens; 1846; property

Section 7 (page 2 of 2) – page 55

11. c. 1845
12. a. Los Angeles
13. c. made California a free state
14. e. 1848
15. a. James Polk
16. Commodore Sloat

John Frémont – surveying party
15 million dollars – Mexican Cession
Manifest Destiny –.U.S. expansion to Pacific Ocean
Ezekiel Merritt – Bear Flag Revolt leader
Rio Grande – Mexico/Texas Boundary
"California Republic" – new flag
Compromise of 1850 – free state

Section 9 – page 69

1. fortune seeker
2. around the southern tip of South America; through the isthmus of Panama; across the Oregon Trail
3. At American river in the Sacramento Valley near Sutter's sawmill
4. *Teacher Check*
   1848; gold; Sutter's; Sacramento Valley; year; around the world; California; February 28, 1849; hundreds; gold-hungry; abandoned; gold; population; 20,000; 107,000; small town; large city; people; 1850

Section 7 (page 1 of 2) – page 54

1. *Teacher Check*
2. *Teacher Check*
3. declare war on Mexico
4. recognize Texas' independence
5. If Texas was admitted to the Union, Mexico would declare war on the United States
6. CA, UT, NV, NM, WY, CO and part of AZ
7. January 1847; Battle of San Gabriel
8. Would it be a free state or a slave state?
9. control and populate
10. a river boundary between Mexico and Texas

Section 8 – page 62

1. 1850; discovery of gold
2. gold was "lying" in the streets
3. *Teacher Check*
4. They planned on returning to Asia.
5. Whites controlled the job market.
6. *Teacher Check*
7. c. women's work
8. a. fortunes

Section 10 – page 80

1. They wanted a voice in the government.
2. Peter H. Burnett
3. *Teacher Check*
4. the increase in population

September 9, 1850 – California Statehood
State Animal – Grizzly Bear
State Bird – Valley Quail
Sacramento – Permanent State Capital
State Tree – California Redwood
State Mineral – Gold
State Insect – Dog Face Butterfly
Nickname – Golden State
State Flower – Golden Poppy
Monterey – First State Capital
Thirty-first State – California
State Marine Mammal – Gray Whale

California
Early History

Section 11 – page 83
Crossword Puzzle
(Top Right)

Section 11 – page 84
Scrambled Sentence
(Lower Left)

Section 11 – page 85
Word Search
(Lower Right)

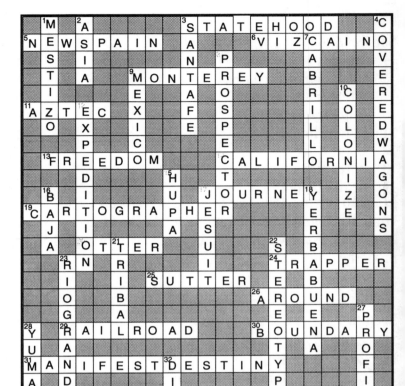

California
Review Activity

Name _____

Date _____

Scrambled Sentences

Write the words in the correct order to make sentences.
(Make sure you *capitalize* the first word of the sentence.)

1.
   The Native Americans were the first people to live in California.
2.
   Mexican Americans were formed by the combination of two nations.
3.
   The kidnapped African people were not ignorant or primitive.
4.
   Francis Drake claimed California for England and named it New Albion.
5.
   The King of Spain ordered settlements to be established in California.
6.
   Many Native Americans left the missions to get more personal freedom.
7.
   President Polk offered Mexico $25 million for California and Rio Grande.
8.
   Chinese sailors reached the American continent as early as 1565.
9.
   Wagon trains usually traveled the Oregon Trail because it was safest.
10.
   California's Constitutional Convention was held in the capital of Monterey.
11.
   In 1854, the capital was permanently moved to Sacramento.
12.
   I learned a lot about California, but am glad this book is finally completed.

LEARNING THE CONTINENTS

Students use maps to identify, memorize and locate the countries, waterways and points of interest on each continent (except Antarctica). Each continent has 16 pages of activities, including a word search for review. *Teacher instructions and keys are included.*

#1906 . . . . 4th-8th

BEST SELLERS

COUNTRY STUDY BOOKS

Each individual country within each respective continent has new words to look up in the dictionary, a large outline map, one page of current facts (population, area, capital, largest city, flag w/description, additional interesting information, and more), one or two pages of history and a page of review questions at the end of each country's section. *Teacher instructions and answer keys are included.*

No. AMERICA #1965 . . . . 4th-8th
So. AMERICA #1975 . . . . 4th-8th
FAR EAST #1935 . . . . 4th-8th
MIDDLE EAST #1936 . . . . 4th-8th
CANADA #1985 . . . . 4th-8th

❖   ❖   ❖

CONTINENT MAPS & STUDIES

This book contains Outline, Waterway, Political Boundary Map and Individual Fact Sheet for all of the continents. (Antarctica only has fact sheet and outline map.) There are questions, research activities and a glossary that can be used with each continent. *Teacher instructions and keys are included.*

#1905 . . . . 4th-8th

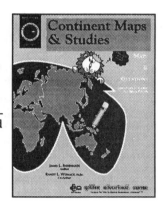

❖   ❖   ❖

CALIFORNIA & WASHINGTON

California Early History: This is a simplified, yet complete, resource book detailing the history of California through statehood. This tremendous resource includes sections on the contributions made by Native Americans, Asians, Africans and Mexicans to the growth and development of the state. Review questions and bonus activities follow each section. *94 pages; Teacher instructions and keys are included.*

California Geography:
Students are given a world overview with a specific review of California's climate and its physical, economic and political features. Lessons are reinforced with maps, exercises, review questions and bonus activities. *63 pages; Teacher instructions and answer keys are included.*

Washington Geography: Identical to California, but with Washington state information. *63 pages; Teacher instructions and answer keys are included.*

CALIFORNIA EARLY HISTORY #2911 . . . . 4th-8th
CALIFORNIA GEOGRAPHY #2911 . . . . 4th-8th
WASHINGTON GEOGRAPHY #2601 . . . . 4th-8th

U.S. STUDIES   **BEST SELLERS**

U.S. Outline Maps: This book has an individual fact sheet and outline map for each of the 50 states, Washington, D.C. and the entire United States. U.S. waterways and state boundary maps are also included. There are also individual question and research pages that can be used with each of the states.
110 pages with teacher instructions

U.S. Geography: Each section of this book begins with new vocabulary words to look up and define. The sections simply cover a world's overview, physical, economic, political and climatic features of the U.S. Maps, activities, questions and review questions are included in each section.
63 pages; Teacher instructions and answer keys are included.

Complete Book of U.S. State Studies: **NEW**
This book includes the same sections as in the *U.S. Outline Maps* book listed above. It also includes historical information about the Native Americans living in the region before any settlers came, as well as the early settlers up to the time of statehood. Each state also has interesting trivia facts and a word search puzzle.
219 pages; Teacher instructions and answer keys are included.

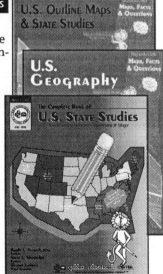

U.S. OUTLINE MAPS #1992 . . . . 4th-8th
U.S. GEOGRAPHY #1993 . . . . 4th-8th
COMPLETE U.S. STATE STUDIES #1995 . . . . 4th-8th

  Golden educational Center
G.E.C. Publications   *"Leading The Way In Creative Educational Materials"* ™

THE BEST EVER BOOK ABOUT
CALIFORNIA MISSIONS

This is a simplified, yet complete, resource book detailing each of the 21 Spanish (Catholic) Missions established along El Camino Real. The book begins with a 14 page historical background section that explains the secular, military, and religious attitudes and situations of Spain and Mexico which were instrumental in the history of California. New vocabulary words, maps, pictures, review questions, and *Bonus Activities* (research questions) are included in this section, as well as each of the individual mission sections.

Each individual mission section includes a diagram of the mission layouts, a fact sheet explaining the mission's design and compound, two-four pages detailing the historical founding of the mission through secularization, a puzzle (crossword, word search, etc.) relating to the respective mission, and one page about the mission today. Pictures, diagrams, and maps are included in each section. Review questions and bonus (research) activities follow each section. (See the back of this sheet.)

This book also has a section of *Extras*:

1. A map showing the various California Indian tribal regions.

2. A map for the students to complete showing the location of the missions.

3. Pictures of the missions (and/or the campanario) for the students to label.

4. Current addresses and phone numbers.

5. A founding date/information page.

6. Listing of other missions founded in Baja California.

7. An historical time line of California from 1450 to 1850 (statehood).

8. An historical summary of the establishment of the missions.

9. A page listing the various hardships each mission faced.

10. Several pages of craft ideas relating to the missions.

220 reproducible pages;
Teacher instructions, list of additional resources, glossary and answer keys are provided.

THE BEST EVER
CALIFORNIA MISSIONS POSTER MAP

Full-color, totally cool, 17"x22", laminated poster shows each California Mission, the California Indian Tribal Regions are numbered and color coded on the map. There are four reproducible activity pages on the back of the poster.

Every teacher should have this poster displayed in the classroom.

California Missions

Sorry!
The file is too large to print with the each mission picture. Trust us, they are the best quality possible.

The background color and photos match the missions book.

1. Achumawi
2. Atsugewi
3. Cahto
4. Cahuilla
5. Chemehuevi
6. Chilula
7. Chimariko
8. Chumash
9. Costanoan
10. Cupeño
11. Esselen
12. Gabrielino
13. Halchidhoma
14. Hupa
15. Ipai
16. Juana (Juaneño)
17. Karok
18. Kitanemuk
19. Konkow
20. Koso
21. Lassik
22. Luiseño
23. Maidu
24. Mattole
25. Miwok, Interior
26. Miwok, Coastal
27. Miwok, Lake
28. Modoc
29. Mohave
30. Monache
31. Mono
32. Nisenan
33. Nomlaki
34. Nongatl
35. Paiute
36. Patwin
37. Pomo
38. Salinan
39. Serrano
40. Shasta
41. Sinkyone
42. Tataviam
43. Tipai
44. Tolowa
45. Tubatulabal
46. Vanyumi
47. Wailaki
48. Wappo
49. Washo
50. Whilkut
51. Wintu
52. Wiyot
53. Yana
54. Yokuts, Foothill
55. Yokuts, Northern
56. Yokuts, Southern (Tulare)
57. Yuki
58. Yuma
59. Yurok